# Richmond's
## Leigh Street Armory
## & African American Militia

Roice D. Luke, Maureen Elgersman Lee & Stacy L. Burrs

*Photography by Karl Elchinger;
Captions by CW2 John W. Listman Jr., VaARNG (Ret.)*

Published by The History Press
Charleston, SC
www.historypress.com

Copyright © 2018 by Roice D. Luke, Maureen Elgersman Lee and Stacy L. Burrs
All rights reserved

First published 2018

Manufactured in the United States

ISBN 9781467139236

Library of Congress Control Number: 2017963927

*Notice*: The information in this book is true and complete to the best of our knowledge. It is offered without guarantee on the part of the authors or The History Press. The authors and The History Press disclaim all liability in connection with the use of this book.

All rights reserved. No part of this book may be reproduced or transmitted in any form whatsoever without prior written permission from the publisher except in the case of brief quotations embodied in critical articles and reviews.

# Contents

Acknowledgements 5
Introduction: The Battalion and Its Armory 9

1. Virginia's Black Militias: Race, Gender and Power 15
2. The Armories: America's Nineteenth-Century Castles 42
3. The Improbable Leigh Street Armory:
   Jackson Ward, City Politics and a Fighting Editor 62
4. Faithful to the Trust: The Spanish-American War 88
5. A Light Shines in the Darkness: The Armory Lives On 117

Appendix: The Armory Before and After Renovation,
   Photographs by Karl Elchinger 131
Notes 143
Bibliography 151
Index 155
About the Authors 159

# Acknowledgements

As the authors of this book, we have felt a special obligation to tell this important story, an obligation that is as much personal as it is professional. This is because we, together, had the good fortune of being intimately involved in the decision making that led to recently acquiring, preserving, repurposing and, ultimately, opening the Leigh Street Armory as the home of the Black History Museum and Cultural Center of Virginia. As board chairman, board member and executive director, respectively, Stacy Burrs, Roice Luke and Maureen Elgersman Lee worked as an informal planning group, a trifecta of sorts, dedicated to redeveloping the Armory. Jump ahead some years, and the product of that effort is that the Leigh Street Armory is once again, as John Mitchell Jr. portrayed it in 1895, a "beautifully lighted armory" that today can be seen "glowing in magnificent splendor." There are many individuals in various capacities who deserve thanks, so please indulge us over the course of the next few pages.

The Leigh Street Armory would not exist were it not for the bravery and dedication to rights and principles so many displayed more than a century ago. A few individuals played especially important roles as the building's principal champions. They were *Richmond Planet* editor and City Councilman John Mitchell Jr., First Battalion Commander Major W.H. Johnson and City Engineer Colonel W.E. Cutshaw. Credit also goes to the precedent-setting black militia members who clearly were acutely aware that, in those few decades removed from slavery's shadow, they were breaking new ground in serving as citizen soldiers in the Virginia Volunteers.

## Acknowledgements

There are also the largely unrecognized individuals who kept the building's spirit alive after the Armory's conversion to a school. These faculty, staff and administrators continued to serve Richmond's African American children for some eighty years, from 1899 to 1981. And then there were those young black soldiers who, during World War II, spent time recuperating inside the walls of the Armory (then called the Monroe Center) and preparing to move on to war. Like their predecessors in the Virginia Volunteers, they simultaneously asserted their manhood and citizenship by answering the call to serve.

The authors owe a special debt of gratitude as well to the museum's pioneer leaders who first recognized the historic importance of that peerless structure. It was Carroll Anderson Sr., the museum's visionary and founding president, who early in the 1980s recognized that a black history museum had to be established in Richmond and, importantly, that the Armory needed to be preserved and converted into its permanent home. At that time, the museum's founding name was the Virginia Museum for Black History and Archives, Inc. Anderson, his fellow board members and other colleagues launched in 1985 a campaign to raise enough money to fund construction and provide operating support for a few years. However, a fire then destroyed part of the Armory's roof and significantly damaged other parts of the building. It soon became apparent that the cost of renovating the Armory was well beyond their reach.

In the interim, one man, historian and preservationist Selden Richardson, almost single-handedly saved the Armory from being demolished or sold for private use. His efforts, including application to the National and Virginia Historic Registers, ensured that the Armory would live another day. Selden also provided the authors with valuable research materials, photographs and helpful suggestions on this history and on an early draft.

We are especially and personally grateful to the board members who in 2011 embraced a remarkably similar vision for the Leigh Street Armory as had the original board in 1985. The board enthusiastically and unanimously voted to support Stacy Burrs' proposal that the museum once again take responsibility for preserving the historic Leigh Street Armory and converting it into the museum's new home. The board members at that time were Stacy L. Burrs (chair), Dr. Lucille Brown, Dr. Rondle E. Edwards, Dr. Lyle Evans, Rita Garrett Foster, Conaway B. Haskins III, J.W. Robinson Horne, Lisa Johnson-Wright, Jershon I. Jones, Dr. Roice D. Luke, Kevin McLaughlin, Herb Southall, Dr. Inez Tuck, Eugene R. Vango, Bessida Cauthorne White and James Elwood Wright.

## Acknowledgements

Some of the aforementioned board members continued on after 2011; others departed and fresh, new talent joined in. The added board members over the years of development and construction include Marilyn West (chair), Latoya Asia, Kiana Bachaus, Mark N. Brady, Wendy DeGroat, Tina Dickerson, Christina S. Draper, Leonard Edloe, Todd A. Elliott, Kym Grinnage, Dr. Monroe Harris, David Holland, Brian Jackson, Kiana Jamison, Darius Johnson, Brenda A. Jones, Jon King, Penny J. McPherson, Alfred T. Orendorff, Saundra Rollins, Hossein Sadid, Kerryn Sherrod, Levette B. Smiley, Jeff Wilson, Kimberly J. Wilson and Richard Woodward. These all successfully moved the project forward, culminating in the museum's opening on May 5, 2016. We thank them all.

We reserve and herein extend a special thanks to one individual who ensured that the museum continue functioning throughout the many unforeseen twists and turns in this period: Mary C. Lauderdale, the museum manager before, during and after the Armory project. Mary is not only the heart and memory of the museum, she has also been a rock of continuity and stability in the midst of the difficult transition that is institutional transformation. Throughout the years she served the museum—as she continues to do today—she has represented the spirit and mission of the total enterprise. And she has served as the face of the museum, doing so much to secure the trust and support of many museum key constituencies and patrons.

We also thank the many individuals who provided encouragement and support as the Black History Museum and Cultural Center of Virginia took on the Leigh Street Armory project. We do not presume to speak for the museum in this regard, but rather focus on those individuals with whom the authors interacted most closely as they worked on the museum project and this book.

At the risk of leaving out the names of many individuals who made particular contributions along the way, we want specifically to mention some to whom we owe a special debt of gratitude. We, of course, thank former mayor Dwight C. Jones, who, with many others in city administration, notably Denise Lawus, endorsed the idea that the museum take over the Armory and supported development efforts.

A number of key individuals provided both strategic and historical guidance on the Armory project and the book specifically, without whose often-extensive contributions the project might not have been a success: Dr. Edward L. Ayers, Elvatrice Parker Belsches, Madge Bemiss, Jean Patterson Boone, the late Raymond H. Boone, Dr. Charlie Bryan, Dr. Lonnie Bunch,

# Acknowledgements

Christy Coleman, Roger Cunningham, Sa'ad El-Amin, Dr. Carmen Foster, John W. Franklin, Evans Hopkins, Bryon Jefferson, Dr. Gregg Kimball, Dr. Lauranett Lee, Bill Martin, Carlton Moffatt, Alex Nyerges, S. Waite Rawls III, Tom Silvestri, Wally Stettinius, Jim Ukrop and John Ulmschneider. We thank them and the many others who gave of their time, resources and wisdom to help.

We also thank those key individuals who played lead roles in transforming the Leigh Street Armory from a sterile, dark and forbidding shell of a building into the beautiful, warm and vibrant space that the community now enjoys as the Black History Museum. We especially thank the leadership team: Burt Pinnock, Mike Hopkins, Chris Sterling, Chaun Burnette, Rick Pilgrim, Bob Riggs, Brent Ward and many, many others, too numerous to be listed here.

We appreciate the specific contributions two individuals made to this book: photographer Karl Elchinger, who, at no cost to the museum, took the cherished pictures of the building before and after construction, and also military historian John W. Listman Jr., who provided the expert and detailed annotations included with the historic images of the black militia companies.

Finally, this book could not have become a reality were it not for the steadfast support of our respective spouses, Nedra Merrick Luke, Dr. Christopher D. Lee and Dr. Lisa Edwards-Burrs. They were valued partners over the long and challenging six-year period in which the museum worked to restore the historic Leigh Street Armory and we worked on this book.

INTRODUCTION

# THE BATTALION AND ITS ARMORY

Many have driven down West Leigh Street in Richmond, Virginia, and glanced at the distinctive red brick building standing at the corner of St. Peter Street. They might have taken in its round and square turrets, terra-cotta decorative features and crenelated rooflines and wondered: What is that interesting building? Why does it look like that? When was it built? Why is it in Jackson Ward? The more observant passerby might have noticed the placard above the gated entrance that reads, "1895—First Battalion Virginia Volunteers, Infantry—1895." That building actually was an armory, which explains its fortress-like appearance. It was one of hundreds built in American cities during the late nineteenth and very early twentieth centuries, but the only one built for an African American battalion.

In the early 1870s, less than a decade after the Confederacy collapsed and slavery ended, the nation's cities began rebuilding the militia units that the Civil War had depleted. Virginia admitted its first all-black company into the Virginia Volunteers in 1872, only seven years after Civil War hostilities ceased. It combined four Richmond-area companies to form the First Battalion ("colored") in 1876. Throughout those years, other black militia companies and a second battalion formed in communities across Virginia and in other states as well.

American cities also built hundreds of large, formidable and costly armories in which the militia members would train and prepare for emergencies. These armories, however, were not the same as their

# Introduction

*Left*: The Armory on St. Peter and Leigh Streets. *Karl Elchinger, photographer. Black History Museum and Cultural Center of Virginia.*

*Below*: The Armory placard: First Battalion Virginia Volunteers, Infantry, 1895. *Selden Richardson.*

## Introduction

predecessors. They were far grander in their scale, cost and use. Rather than using armories to serve as centers for manufacturing and storing firearms and ammunition, American cities built the later armories to be militia meeting and training centers and to defend local militia members against community outbreaks of violence. In their day, those massive structures were prominent emblems of community celebration and expressions of American patriotism. Across America, gallantly regaled militia companies, battalions and regiments led out from their armories to march in city streets to the beat of military bands and the clattering of prancing horses mounted by finely costumed militia officers. Such was also the case for Richmond's black militia battalion and its armory.

Just imagine regimented black officers and soldiers marching to the beat of a battalion band from the front door of the magnificent Leigh Street Armory. Or imagine the spectacle of Richmond's African American citizens lining the streets and cheering an extended and slow-moving line of black soldiers, community leaders, church officials, fraternal order members, school groups and bands as they paraded celebrating the Fourth of July or Emancipation Day. Imagine, also, the reactions of peering and uneasy white citizens as the children of the once enslaved rehearsed intricate military maneuvers by command of imperious black militia officers on Richmond's Monument Avenue or other city streets. For Richmond's black community, such imagery provided hope-filled confirmation that freedom, equality and full citizenship for them might actually be attainable. The soldiers' highly visible participation as militia members signaled a major advance in civic acceptance and engagement and served as a powerful symbol of both African American manhood and citizenship. For the curious observers, however, it likely symbolized a dramatic change in the city's social order, the outcomes of which few could easily have foreseen.

Over the twenty-seven years from 1872 until 1899, the numbers of black militia members grew rapidly, as did their visibility on the streets of the state's major cities. In 1895, the City of Richmond constructed a magnificent armory for the use of its black militia soldiers, who by then had become a full battalion in the Virginia Volunteers. Building the armory was no ordinary political act, however. No other American city had in that period done the same for a black militia unit, which means that Virginia had no peer or model to follow. Virginia in the still more distant past led the nation in the ownership, imprisonment and sale of the ancestors of many of the black Volunteers for whom that armory was built. The creation of the Leigh Street Armory was, by all accounts, unprecedented and improbable. Leigh Street

# Introduction

Armory was unique, not because of any extraordinary architectural features, but for the occupants for whom the city built it. Because of Richmond and Virginia's documented racial past, the Armory stands as a true anomaly in American military and social history.

Unfortunately, the Leigh Street Armory functioned as such for only three and a half years, its life as a military institution ending in the first months of 1899. At that time, not only did Virginia's governor begin the process of disbanding all black militia units, but city officials also converted the building into a segregated elementary school. A series of racial confrontations involving Virginia's African American Volunteers, who had been training for the Spanish-American War, precipitated these developments. So, too, did the broader context of Jim Crow, which at that time was restricting the civil rights of its African American citizens.

The Leigh Street Armory has evaded demolition and, with some timely intervention, has survived the ravages of time. Its grandeur has been preserved, making it a highly visible vestige of an era long passed. Yes, the military still builds armories, but these in very few respects resemble the magnificence of the late nineteenth-century structures the cities erected as monuments to a time when the militias were central to the social order. The United States no longer uses armories to defend against dissent and disruption in its cities. Nor does it operate government-organized militia units, despite the attention given them by the Constitution and the Second Amendment. And many of the grand armories the cities built for them have since been either demolished or adapted for other uses. To understand the place of the nineteenth-century militia and their armories, one must view them through a social/cultural prism. They were far more than mere extensions of the military; they were cultural icons, a point that was especially true for Richmond's black militia battalion, as well as its magnificent Leigh Street Armory.

## Framing the Book

This book discusses a historically significant, one-of-a-kind historic building and the battalion for which it was built. But it also examines a component of American history that, though central to early American concepts of defense and community, no longer factors into modern society. It also unveils a host of other interconnected elements that were unique to that period when the United States transitioned from the loathsome institution of slavery to

# Introduction

its unfortunate offspring, Jim Crow. In exploring the sequence of events surrounding the formation of Virginia's African American militia, the First Battalion's struggle to secure funding for its armory and the extraordinary race-based conflicts the black Volunteers experienced while at camp training for the Spanish-American War, the book lays bare some of the racial tensions the nation faced as it approached the dawn of the twentieth century. This was truly a time of sorting on matters of race, gender and civil rights.

We begin the story of Richmond's First Battalion of Virginia Volunteers by placing it in its larger historical context. To do this, we assess the place of militias in America's military structure and the emergence of Virginia black militia units after the Civil War. We then examine the reasons why American cities built such costly armories for their local militia units and how black and white leaders together made it possible for Richmond to be the only city in America to construct an armory for its black militia members. We close the story by reviewing the gripping, but discouraging, events that enveloped Richmond's black Volunteers as they sought to express their patriotism and honor by serving in the Spanish-American War. Unfortunately, events at the intersection of race, gender and power robbed these men of the glory they had expected. These events also contributed to the state's decision to disband the black militia units and repurpose the Leigh Street Armory. Finally, we reflect on the Armory's post-militia history and its long-overdue return to glory as a monument to the history and resilience of the very people for whom it was constructed—the African American community of Richmond, in particular, and of Virginia at large.

The story of the First Battalion and its magnificently built armory is also a vehicle that allows the voices of various people, including John Mitchell Jr., Major Joseph B. Johnson and the Volunteers themselves, to be heard. In some cases, we have excerpted those voices; other times we have presented them without truncation. This is by design and helps convey Richmond's late nineteenth-century zeitgeist while making the case for the importance of these courageous Virginians who spoke truth to power.

The story of the rise and fall of Virginia's black Volunteer soldiers and their armory is, therefore, as much about hope and expectation as it is of despair. It is also very much a story that is truly emblematic of that all-important transition period between the fall of slavery and the steady, sometimes imperceptible erosion of freedoms and opportunity that Jim Crow imposed upon America's black citizenry for almost one hundred years. For much the same reasons, the black militias also experienced an almost simultaneous exhilaration, followed by tarnished reputations and dashed hopes.

CHAPTER 1

# VIRGINIA'S BLACK MILITIAS

*Race, Gender and Power*

American historiography tells the story of Paul Revere and the other brave minutemen who, in mid-April 1775, challenged the red-coated British at Lexington and Concord, Massachusetts. Those minutemen were actually militia men, whom many in the Revolutionary period considered the foundation of America's military structure. The government (first Britain, then the newly formed United States of America) could call these often-reluctant citizen warriors to battle whenever the need for this might arise. The militias contributed importantly in the colonial era, in the Revolutionary War and in all of the nation's wars through to the end of the nineteenth century. George Washington himself gained important military experience while serving as adjutant general of the British-organized Virginia militia.[1]

The term militia derives from the word "milite," which means soldiers. However, militia members were not professional fighters, but able-bodied civilians upon whom their countries relied in times of need. They tended to be organized around cities and villages, since transportation and communication between communities made it difficult for a national, full-time army to provide essential and urgent protection. Because they were not professional fighters, America's late eighteenth- to late nineteenth-century militia members were often poorly trained and lacked needed and updated military equipment and provisions. Being volunteers, they also tended to lack the commitment needed to engage in military conflict. With a few notable exceptions, they proved themselves relatively ineffective as a fighting force,

George Washington as colonel in the Virginia Regiment, 1772. *Wikimedia Commons.*

especially when compared to the better trained and equipped, but more costly, standing armies.[2]

Even George Washington, who relied on the militias to build up his troops during the Revolutionary War, had serious misgivings about their competence. He said:

Minutemen fight in the Battle of Lexington. *Library of Congress.*

> *To place any* [dependence] *upon Militia, is, assuredly, resting upon a broken staff. Men just dragged from the tender Scenes of* [domestic] *life; unaccustomed to the din of Arms; totally unacquainted with every kind of Military skill, which being followed by a want of confidence in themselves, when opposed to Troops regularly* [trained], *disciplined, and appointed, superior in knowledge, and superior in Arms, makes them timid, and ready to fly from their own shadows.*[3]

## THE MILITIAS AND THE CONSTITUTION

The limitations of the militias notwithstanding, the framers of the Constitution considered them so important that they wrote them explicitly into Articles I and II of the Constitution, the sections that laid out congressional and presidential powers.

Recognizing that the militias alone could not provide for the nation's defense, the founding fathers also wrote a standing army and navy into the Constitution. Few are aware that the first sentence in Article II of the Constitution not only designates the president as "Commander in Chief of the Army and Navy of the United States," but also "of the Militia of the several States, when called into the actual Service of the United States." The latter role, of course, continues into the present day, as the president is now the commander in chief of what the militias became—the National Guard. Understanding the differences between militias and a standing army and navy, the founders assigned the states responsibility for establishing and managing the militia units. The federal government would take charge only when they were called into actual national service.

Given the bifurcated governance and the distinctive function of the militias versus the army and navy, the framers found it necessary to devote additional constitutional text to the militias. Specifically, they sought to clarify their unique roles in supporting the interests of the states. To ensure the continuance of the militias as local protectors (e.g., in the South, to defend against slave uprisings), they also wrote the militias and their right to bear arms into the Bill of Rights' Second Amendment.

The clause in the Constitution that spells out the purposes of the militias is especially illuminating, as it assigned them three roles. The first role "to execute the Laws of the Union" and the second to "suppress Insurrections" were more consistent with community policing. The third role to "repel Invasions" assigned to militias a more military purpose—that they be available when the president called on them to protect the nation. Recognizing the need for divided governance over the militias, the Constitution assigned to the Congress responsibility for "organizing, arming, and disciplining, the Militia, and for governing such Part of them as may be employed in the Service of the United States." The Constitution also assigned to the states responsibility for overseeing and managing the militias when they were *not* called on in war. The states would be responsible for "the Appointment of the Officers, and the Authority of training the Militia according to the discipline prescribed by Congress"—again, when not called into actual national service.

Six months after the nation ratified the Bill of Rights, Congress passed two bills—the First and Second Militia Acts of 1792—that further clarified militia roles and procedures. These specified who should serve in the militias, when they would be placed in the nation's service and how they were to be organized and governed. Of interest is the clause that dealt with race: the militias were to be composed of "each and every free able-bodied white male citizen of the respective States." It further specified who was to be called: a male citizen "who is or shall be of age of eighteen years, and under the age of forty-five years."[4] As a result, few blacks served in America's wars, and no blacks served in the state militias, from that point until Reconstruction. Virginia's governments also restricted blacks' access to weapons from the early seventeenth century through the end of the Civil War. In 1639–40, for

George Washington as commander-in-chief. *Library of Congress.*

instance, the General Assembly ruled that "ALL persons except negroes to be provided with arms and ammunition."⁵

The militia's role to suppress insurrections became especially important in the South during slavery. They were, in effect, the indispensable arms of city and state governments for protecting white citizens and property

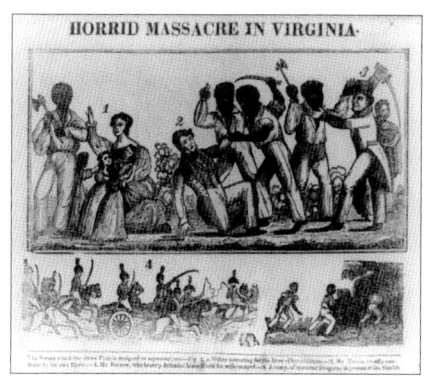

Title page for *Nat Turner Confessions*, Richmond, Virginia, circa 1832. *Library of Congress.*

against organized internal threats, most especially from the possibility of slave uprisings, whether actual or rumored. The militias also assisted in the conduct of slave patrols in the South that tracked down runaway slaves. The need for militias in the South thus engendered considerable support for them within the white community, for arming them and for the Second Amendment.

The Haitian Revolution that began in 1791 not only produced the free republic of Haiti in 1804 but also spread ripples of fear throughout southern white communities in the United States, galvanizing great public support for strengthening and arming militias. Three homegrown slave rebellions exacerbated those fears in Virginia and elsewhere and generated corresponding support for the militias in the decades preceding the Civil War. In 1800, Gabriel of the Prosser plantation planned an invasion of Richmond, but the failed slave rebellion was betrayed to authorities and quelled by the state militia. Nat Turner's 1831 rebellion in Southampton, Virginia, led to the deaths of sixty whites before local militias captured Turner and his co-conspirators. Finally, John Brown's 1859 raid on the federal arsenal at Harpers Ferry was suppressed by militias but was yet another ominous event in the ever-present question about slavery's future in Virginia and the United States.[6]

## BLACK MILITARY SERVICE AND THE CONSTITUTION

Some African Americans did carry weapons and fought on the sides of both Revolutionary and British forces. For the most part, however, the military used black soldiers to perform menial tasks and to serve in nonfighting roles, such as fifers, drummers and body servants. Despite the racial prohibition of the 1791 law, African Americans did serve in most of America's wars in the nineteenth century, mostly in limited numbers and roles. A small number served in the U.S. Navy in the War of 1812, for instance, due in part to the shortage of naval manpower.

The largest contingent of African Americans to fight for their country in that century occurred in the Civil War. Political considerations were key to their limited use in the early stages of the war. At that point, Lincoln was concerned that the enlistment of blacks could motivate the border states to switch sides and join the Confederacy. Pressures for emancipation, rising shortages of manpower and the rapidly growing availability of escaped slaves (or "contraband"), however, became increasingly important in the president's thinking as the war progressed.

Congress passed the 1861 and 1862 Confiscation Acts and the 1862 Militia Act, which linked military service to freedom for contraband exslaves. Via the preliminary Emancipation Proclamation of September 1862, Lincoln announced plans to emancipate all persons enslaved within Confederate states or parts thereof still in rebellion on January 1, 1863. On that New Year's Day, Lincoln declared those enslaved persons "forever free." The prospect of proving their dedication to the Union and gaining freedom attracted many blacks into the military in the final two years of the Civil War. By its end, nearly 180,000 African Americans served in the army and some 20,000 served in the navy.[7]

Company E, Fourth U.S. Colored Infantry, circa 1864. *Library of Congress*.

*The Hope of Emancipation* by Thomas Nast. *Library of Congress.*

Freedmen Village, Hampton, Virginia, 1865. *Library of Congress.*

Freedmen family, Richmond, Virginia, 1865. *Library of Congress.*

On July 25, 1868, *Harper's Weekly* published an astonishing cartoon that American artist and illustrator Alfred Waud used to showcase the Freedmen's Bureau's role in facilitating African Americans' difficult transition from slavery to freedom. This particular cartoon portrayed a soldier serving with the Freedmen's Bureau standing between angry black and white mobs. As the journal put it, "The *Harper's Weekly* editor agreed with cartoonist Waud's perspective that the Freedmen's Bureau had prevented a 'war of races' in the postwar South…stepping between the hostile parties and saying to them, with irresistible authority, 'Peace!'"[8] The interesting thing is the cartoon showed both mobs, black and white, angrily brandishing swords and rifles. Published only three years after slavery's end, this may be one of the first visual depictions in American history of blacks exercising their confirmed Second Amendment right as citizens to keep and bear arms.

The Radical Republicans who dominated Congress during and right after the Civil War worked to ensure that black Americans, once freed from the threat of enslavement, could enjoy rights guaranteed for white citizens. They passed key federal statutes and amendments to the Constitution, among which were the Freedmen's Bureau Acts (1865 through to 1872), the Civil Rights Act (1866) and, ultimately, the critically important Reconstruction Amendments to the Constitution. The Thirteenth Amendment outlawed slavery in the United States except as a punishment for crime. The Fourteenth defined citizenship and promised equal protection of the laws. And the Fifteenth Amendment prohibited race, color and previous slave status from being used as legitimate barriers to male suffrage. Notably, the 1866 Freedmen's Bureau legislation specifically

"The Freedmen's Bureau" agent between armed blacks and whites, published in *Harper's Weekly*, July 1868. *Library of Congress.*

sought to protect for the freedmen "any of the civil rights or immunities belonging to white persons, including…the constitutional right of bearing arms."[9]

In 1866, Congress also sought to provide African Americans greater access to the military by adding six black regiments to the army. Nearly three thousand black veterans of the Civil War took advantage of this perceived opportunity to express their rights as citizens and reenlisted, only to find themselves serving under the leadership of white officers. Many more black Americans, however, opted to join militia groups that states at that time were forming. By 1880, half of the then thirty-eight states in the nation had formed black militia companies.[10]

At the conclusion of the Civil War, the states' constitutionally assigned role to appoint and train militia officers placed governors in highly sensitive positions when dealing with the country's long-standing racial divisions. This became important in Virginia and other southern states at the beginning of the Spanish-American War (1898–99), when governors had to decide whether black volunteers, many of whom were members of militia companies, would be able to serve, to be integrated with white units and to have officers of their own race.

# Richmond's Leigh Street Armory & African American Militia

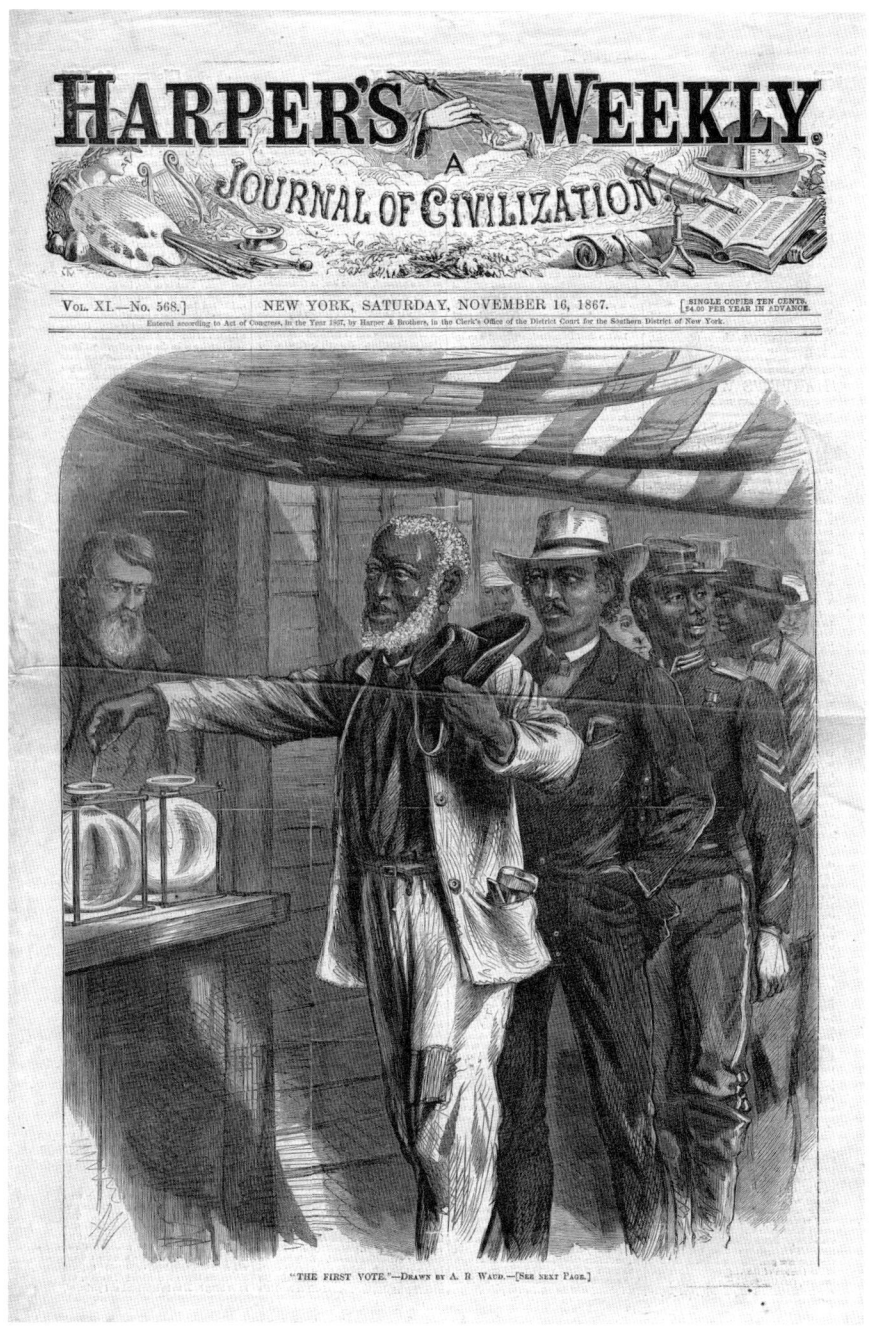

"The First Vote" by A.R. Wauld, in *Harper's Weekly*, November 16, 1867. *Library of Congress.*

Such were the post–Civil War issues that the Fourteenth Amendment's equal protection clause was designed to address: "No State shall…deny to any person within its jurisdiction the equal protection of the laws." However, in the ensuing years following passage of the Fourteenth Amendment, considerable differences remained within the government as to how that amendment should be interpreted. Of particular relevance to this was the regrettable *Plessy v. Ferguson* (1896) decision that protected separate but equal as part of the police power of the states. The Supreme Court handed down the *Plessy* decision barely one year after Richmond built the Leigh Street Armory and two years before the Spanish-American War began. Importantly, the Fourteenth Amendment played an important role in Virginia when the governor stewed over whether to recruit black soldiers and, if so, whether to allow them to have their own black officers.

## Virginia's Black Militias

In the years between 1872 and 1899, Virginia led the nation in establishing black militia units and securing appointments for black officers. The exact numbers of Virginia companies and volunteers is unclear. In part, this is because some black companies over the years formed, others disbanded and still others combined with existing units. While the numbers shifted over time, by 1880, Virginia had in place approximately twenty black companies and around 170 black officers appointed to lead them.[11] From the mid-1880s and through the 1890s, the number of black companies steadily declined. Financial burdens associated with maintaining rented facilities, acquiring needed uniforms and equipment and sustaining training and exercises all proved to be major challenges for the black volunteers. This was especially true since the units were made up primarily of working-class, low-income men.[12]

Across the post–Civil War South, unofficial black militia units formed in some communities, primarily to ensure black self-protection from white men angered by the Confederacy's collapse. In his review of black military history in Virginia, Bruce A. Glasrud noted:

> *In Richmond after the war, some black veterans may have formed unofficial militia units, in part for self-protection, and such groups apparently marched in an Emancipation Day parade on April 3, 1866,*

| TABLE 1. AFRICAN AMERICAN MILITIA COMPANIES IN THE VIRGINIA VOLUNTEERS | | | |
|---|---|---|---|
| UNIT | LOCATION | DATE ORGANIZED | DATE DISBANDED |
| Attucks Guard | Richmond | Feb. 17, 1872 | Jan. 26, 1899+ |
| Carney Guard | Richmond | Mar. 18, 1873 | Jan. 26, 1899+ |
| Union Guard | Richmond | Jun. 12, 1873 | May 14, 1891 |
| Petersburg Guard | Petersburg | Jun. 25, 1873 | Jan. 26, 1899+ |
| Langston Guard | Norfolk | Nov. 7, 1873 | Jan. 26, 1899+ |
| Virgina Greys/ Rich. Light Inf. | Richmond | April 17, 1874 | April 12, 1887 |
| Virginia Guard | Portsmouth | Nov. 9, 1875 | May 7, 1888 |
| Seaboard Elliott Greys | Portsmouth | Jan. 28, 1876 | Feb. 26, 1887 |
| Libby Guard | Hampton | Dec. 21, 1876 | May 7, 1888 |
| Hill City Guard | Lynchburg | Oct. 5, 1877 | May 20, 1889 |
| Virginia Guard | Lynchburg | Feb. 27, 1878 | Feb. 20, 1889 |
| Petersburg Blues | Petersburg | May 7, 1878 | Jan. 26, 1899+ |
| State Guard | Richmond | May 14, 1878 | Jan. 26, 1899+ |
| Flipper Guard | Petersburg | Oct. 29, 1878 | Jan. 26, 1899+ |
| National Guard | Norfolk | Jan. 28, 1879 | Jan. 26, 1899+ |
| Hannibal Guard | Danville | Feb. 5, 1879 | Oct. 10, 1887 |
| Douglas Guard | Danville | Feb. 5, 1879 | Aug. 24, 1883 |
| Hannibal Guard | Norfolk | Feb. 21, 1880 | May 7, 1888 |
| Garfield Light Inf. (Blues) | Fredericksburg | Mar. 30, 1882 | Nov. 21, 1895 |
| Staunton Light Inf. | Staunton | Jul. 10, 1882 | May 7, 1888 |
| + indicates service as a company in the Sixth Virginia Volunteers during the Spanish-American War, 1898–99. | | | |

Transcribed from the *Virginia GuardPost* (Winter 1995): 12.

*and again on July 4. In May 1867, Major General John M. Schofield, commander of the First Military District, ordered one unit, the Lincoln Mounted Guard, to be disbanded when its members refused to obey segregation laws on a streetcar.*[13]

In 1870, the first "official" black company in Virginia formed and named itself the Attucks Guard, named for Crispus Attucks, an African American whom many consider the first casualty of the Revolutionary War. This was the same year Congress passed an act allowing Virginia to seat its senators and representatives in Washington, D.C. The state then formed the Virginia Volunteers in 1871 and, a year later, authorized black soldiers to join the Volunteers. The Attucks Guard thus became the first black unit accepted into the Volunteers in 1872. The state organized the First Battalion of Virginia Volunteers in 1876 and the Second Battalion in 1881. Various efforts to organize the remaining black companies into battalions and to combine battalions into a regiment failed, due in part to insufficient resources being available to facilitate coordination of companies across the state.[14]

Military historian John Listman Jr. has suggested that the officer issue also factored into the decision not to move forward with forming a black regiment in Virginia. This is because a black regiment would require the appointment of blacks to ranks above that of major, something white officers and soldiers opposed. Unfortunately, a direct consequence of the failure to form a black regiment is that company officers received little, if any, oversight from field officers. As a result, discipline among the troops suffered.

Making matters worse, black militia units frequently received old, outdated weapons. In 1885, five black companies used Civil War–era muzzleloading rifles; the Staunton Light Guard was not armed at all. According to military historian Roger Cunningham, the black militia members represented about 30 percent of the Virginia Volunteers but had access to only about 6 percent of the state's best weapons.[15]

The formation of the First Battalion in 1876 combined four Richmond companies: Attucks Guard, Carney Guard, State Guard and Virginia Greys/Richmond Light Infantry (disbanded in 1887) and the Union Guard from Manchester, which at that time was a separate city from Richmond. In those years, as Listman noted, the state segregated the militia units by race. Consistent with this, the state referred to the First Battalion as the "First Battalion, Infantry (Colored)." Sometimes they used the word "separate," Listman noted, in place of the more explicit and racialized term "colored."[16]

The state appointed R.H. Johnson of the Carney Guard to the rank of major and assigned him to serve as battalion commander. Six years later, in 1882, Johnson resigned from this position, and in his place, the state appointed J.B. Johnson of Manchester's Union Guard to the rank of major and appointed him battalion commander. During the Spanish-American War, J.B. Johnson also served as major over the First Battalion within the Sixth Virginia Regiment. This appointment began in June 1898 and ended

# Richmond's Leigh Street Armory & African American Militia

African American Crispus Attucks, the first martyr of the Revolutionary War, killed at the 1770 Boston Massacre. Engraved by Paul Revere. *Wikimedia.*

The Attucks Guard of Richmond at the National Encampment in Washington, D.C., May 1887. *U.S. Army Heritage and Education Center.*

The First and Second Battalion officers as of 1895, from the report of the adjutant general of Virginia, 1895, p. 23–24. *Black History Museum and Cultural Center of Virginia.*

in the spring of 1899, when Johnson and his battalion returned home from the training camps and the battalion disbanded.

Five years after formation of the First Battalion, in 1881, Virginia joined five companies, two from Portsmouth and three from Petersburg, to form the Second Battalion. William H. Palmer became major and commander of the Second Battalion, in which capacity he served until his death in 1887. Virginia reorganized the Second Battalion in 1891 and in 1895 (the year the Armory was constructed) appointed W.H. Johnson to serve as major and battalion commander over the Second. Similar to J.B. Johnson, W.H. Johnson served as major over the Second Battalion within the Sixth Virginia Regiment during the early part of troop training for the Spanish-American War. After only a few months in this role, however, he and his fellow officers of the Second Battalion resigned their positions in protest, the white regiment and other camp leaders having challenged their qualifications and appointed white officers in their place. As with the First Battalion, Virginia disbanded the Second in the spring of 1899.[17]

Major William Henry Johnson, commander of the Second Battalion at Camp Poland, Tennessee, 1898. *Virginia State University.* "Note he is wearing gaiters (leggings) over his shoes, not cavalry boots, although he had to serve on a horse in his official duties." *Caption by John W. Listman Jr.*

TABLE 2.

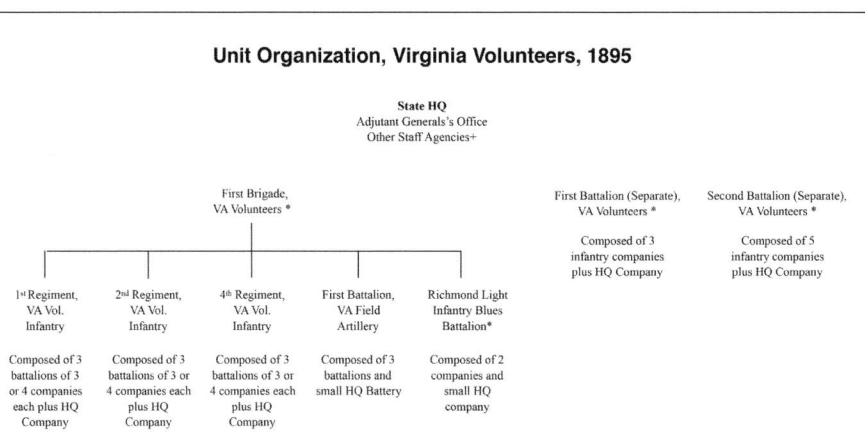

**Unit Organization, Virginia Volunteers, 1895**

**State HQ**
Adjutant Generals's Office
Other Staff Agencies+

- First Brigade, VA Volunteers *
  - 1st Regiment, VA Vol. Infantry — Composed of 3 battalions of 3 or 4 companies each plus HQ Company
  - 2nd Regiment, VA Vol. Infantry — Composed of 3 battalions of 3 or 4 companies each plus HQ Company
  - 4th Regiment, VA Vol. Infantry — Composed of 3 battalions of 3 or 4 companies each plus HQ Company
  - First Battalion, VA Field Artillery — Composed of 3 battalions and small HQ Battery
  - Richmond Light Infantry Blues Battalion* — Composed of 2 companies and small HQ company
- First Battalion (Separate), VA Volunteers * — Composed of 3 infantry companies plus HQ Company
- Second Battalion (Separate), VA Volunteers * — Composed of 5 infantry companies plus HQ Company

\* The last cavalry troop (in this case "troop" being the equivalent of an infantry company) in state service, the Ashby Light Horse, was converted and redesignated in 1894 as Company B, Richmond Light Infantry Blues (RLIB). On 1 May 1894 it was consolidated with Company A, RLIB (formerly an element of the 1st VA Infantry), to organize the Richmond Light Infantry Blues Battalion. This battalion was, like the two black battalions, separate from any higher regimental structure; however, unlike the two black battalions it reported to the commanding general, First Brigade, VA Vol. The two black battalions were not included in the organization of the First Brigade so their commanders, each a major, reported directly to the Adjutant General of Virginia, with no intervening chain of command.

+ At the time the State Headquarters of the Virginia Volunteers had rudimentary departments for Adjutant, Judge Advocate, Quartermaster and State Inspector plus a couple of civilian ladies to do paperwork. Obtaining the services such as medical (to include doctors and what we today would call medical corpsmen), veterinarians (remember everything was still dependent on horse/mule power), black smiths, trainers, etc., were the responsibility of the regimental commanders to recruit themselves. This is an area where the black units suffered from not being assigned to a higher HQ, they had little if any access to such specialized people. The Second Battalion did have at least one doctor prior to being mobilized in 1898, but it is unknown if the First Battalion did. Neither apparently had any horses prior to the mobilization so they probably had no vets. Both are documented as having chaplains in the 1890s.

Compiled by CW2 John W. Listman, Jr. Historian, VaARNG (Ret.), February 2017

Captain William Henry Johnson and unknown first sergeant of the Petersburg Blues, Company C, Second Battalion, circa 1890. *Virginia State University.* "Johnson is wearing the Model 1872 officer pattern forge cap and heavily braided overcoat. The sergeant is wearing the Model 1886 cork helmet with brass eagle plate and spike. His cadet gray overcoat has the removable cape then popular in the Army." *Caption by John W. Listman Jr.*

It is interesting to compare the upbringing of these latter two notable nineteenth-century black commanders. Major J.B. Johnson of the First Battalion was a descendant of free blacks in Virginia. At the time he served as major, he worked as a mechanic. W.H. Johnson of the Second Battalion, by contrast, was born in slavery, lived in Petersburg and, when appointed major, was a school principal. One can only wonder how such differences might have contributed to their respective rises within the ranks and to their places in the ensuing conflicts while at camp during the Spanish-American War.[18]

## THE BLACK MILITIA UNITS SERVE AT THE STATE LEVEL

Wary mayors and governors nationally avoided calling on their black militia companies to enforce the peace, in part out of concern that their presence might incite race-based reactions from black citizens, white citizens or both. Despite this concern, as Cunningham pointed out, Virginia appears to have engaged black troops in five situations. State officials limited blacks' roles, but the level of involvement still exceeded what any other states had done.

First, in response to blacks rioting in Petersburg in 1873, Virginia's governor, at the request of Petersburg's mayor, ordered both black and white militia troops to be ready in case they were needed. Though they were not called upon to serve at this time, the troops won compliments for their quick and orderly response to the crisis. Cunningham reported, "The *Petersburg Index-Appeal* commended the men of the Petersburg Guard for doing their duty 'as faithful citizens and true soldiers,' and said that 'it affords us more than ordinary satisfaction to assure our people that in this organization they have an element of the colored people that may always be relied upon to aid in the maintenance of law and order.'"[19]

Such responses, combined with the general orderly and patriotic way in which the black troops functioned within their units, helped to soften worries over black militia participation. It is notable that this particular activation of black troops occurred a year after the first black militia group, Richmond's Attucks Guard, officially joined the Virginia Volunteers.

The second event occurred thirteen years later. In late August 1886, a major earthquake centered in Charleston, South Carolina, spread structural damage from Atlanta to Richmond. On the night of August 31, 1886,

Richmond's state penitentiary experienced major damage. As the walls shook, prisoners shouted out in fear, some walls fell and a few prisoners escaped. Richmond's black Carney Guard was among the first militia units to respond to the mayor's call for help. The guard played an important early role in settling the situation until other troops could assemble and take over.[20]

Third, a few months later, in early January 1887, Virginia's governor called out Richmond's black State Guard along with two white militia companies to restore order at the Newport News shipyard where black workers were rioting:

> *At 4 A.M. today the three companies from Richmond arrived, under the command of General Anderson, and were at once placed on guard. About this time the train arrived with the men on board to take the striker's places. About 10 o'clock work was commenced on the different piers by the new men. The State Guard (colored), Captain Paul, guarded the approaches to the coal pier, while Companies A and R, Captains Spence and Jones, guarded other piers. At 3 P.M. all was quiet.... The major ordered all the bar-rooms to be closed today. The fact that colored troops were sent to the scene created the greatest surprise.*[21]

Fourth, in that same year, a court case involving a white Petersburg doctor who had slapped a black girl greatly heightened tensions within the black community. Concerned about rioting, the Petersburg mayor called out three guard units, one of which was the black Petersburg Guard. Cunningham wrote of this:

> *The Petersburg Guard reported that thirty-nine of its men arrived at their armory within seventy-five minutes of the mayor's ten o'clock order, and they remained under arms until four o'clock.* The Richmond Dispatch

The State Guard of Richmond at the National Encampment in Washington, D.C., May 1887. *U.S. Army Heritage and Education Center.*

*opined that these actions "doubtless had a cooling effect," while a Petersburg newspaper reported that "it is thought by a large number of citizens that the calling out of the military was entirely unnecessary, but the mayor says that nine-tenths of the people think that he acted wisely in so doing."*[22]

Fifth, in January 1888, a fire broke out in the Richmond-based state penitentiary. In response, the prison set off alarms, and prisoners and guards were alerted and activated. Out of concern that things might get out of control, the prison ordered that the military alarm on the roof be sounded. According to the *Richmond Dispatch*, the prison thought that "all the prisoners would have to be marched out of the prison to Monroe Park, or to some lot where they could be securely guarded. All the military, white and colored, cavalry, artillery, and infantry, and all the police responded, giving Superintendent Moses an overwhelming force—but their services were not needed."[23] The black troops helped to calm the crowds that gathered nearby. Among the black units that responded were three from Richmond—State Guard, Carney Guard and Attucks Guard.

## Marching and Ceremony

Throughout the nineteenth century, America's militias became highly ceremonial in their roles and club-like in their structures. Objects of pride in moments of community revelry and celebration, they were grand spectacles when marshaled in full regalia and parading in city streets. This was also true for the black militia units in that period. For the first time in the nation's history, black soldiers marched across the cities with guns on their shoulders and sabers at their sides, providing striking visible confirmation for many that freedom, equality and full citizenship for African Americans might actually be attainable. The black troops marched in a number of inaugural parades for governors and even Presidents Benjamin Harrison in 1881 and Grover Cleveland in 1885. And they traveled to march in various cities, including New York and Boston. More often, they marched to celebrate special local commemorations, including, in particular, Emancipation Day and the Fourth of July.

John Mitchell Jr. frequently reported on the marching of the militia units, portraying in vivid language their gallantry and impressive regalia. The three articles summarized here illustrate the pageantry that often surrounded these events. Noticeably, Mitchell did not pass up an opportunity to feature himself in these and other such articles. And because of his high rank within a prominent black, almost military-appearing fraternal unit, the Knights of Pythias, he featured them (and himself, as a result) in the parades.

The *Planet* published in 1890 the first article to be highlighted here, a full five years before the Armory officially opened for business. The article does refer to an armory that the First Battalion was using. However, since this occurred in 1890, that armory was a rented facility in Richmond. This parade was a major affair, extending two miles. Mitchell was the grand marshal for the parade, in which capacity, among other roles, he ordered the procession to begin. Major Johnson led the First Battalion. The parade was part of the community's commemoration of the Emancipation Proclamation. It specifically celebrated President Abraham Lincoln's initial announcement of the proclamation on September 22, 1862; other emancipation celebrations in Richmond recognized January 1, 1863, as the appropriate date.[24]

It should be noted that many cities and towns across the country debated the best time to celebrate emancipation. This was also true for Richmond. The possibilities included the date of Lincoln's first announcement of the proclamation, on September 22, 1862; the date of the official announcement, on January 1, 1863; the date Richmond fell, on April 3, 1865; the date the nation emancipated Washington, D.C., on April 16, 1862; and the date a major general announced emancipation in Galveston, Texas—known as Juneteenth—on June 19, 1865.

Mention is made in Mitchell's report of various organizations whose names might sound as if they were militia but were not. This included the "horsemen from Henrico Co." and "The Grand Army of the Republic." The horsemen, Mitchell observed, wore "the blue capes of the civilians from the city…[and] presented a fine appearance. They formed the cavalry. The fine Staunton Band headed the procession, discoursing sweet music."[25] In those years, many fraternal organizations wore military-looking dress and used military-sounding titles for ranks and to name their organizational units.

Mitchell noted that "never has there been seen so many colored men on horseback. Every animal was engaged and at times fancy prices were paid."[26] Regarding the horses the militia officers used, because the black militia units had been organized apart from the larger brigade and regimental structures within the Virginia Volunteers, they did not have access to government-funded horses. Nor did they have access to the specialized personnel, such as veterinarians, who would care for them. This required militia members who rode horses in the parade to borrow them from private sources or simply use horses of their own.[27]

These were always grand affairs, embellished by the participants' gallantry and colorful vestments. Mitchell reported that he "wore a light colored slouch-hat, black suit with cream colored satin sash, and was mounted on an iron gray horse." His, of course, was a Knights of Pythias, not a militia, uniform, as Mitchell did not serve in the militia. "A square of mounted police" led out to ensure that they cleared the way for the parade. And "ex-Adjutant A.C. Brown and Capt. Benj. Scott" ensured that the line was orderly and properly maintained. Mitchell also wrote that Scott "had direct control of the civic organizations, and being brought in contact with men who knew nothing of military formations had a time that tried man's soul."[28] Obviously, as he implied, such marchers lacked the military discipline otherwise present in the militia companies to ensure that the line of march remained well formed and orderly.

The militia units were well represented in the parade. Four companies from the First Battalion participated—State Guard, Attucks Guard, Carney Guard and Union Guard from Manchester—as did Petersburg Guard, Flipper Guard and Petersburg Blues, all from Petersburg. Displaying a degree of impatience, Mitchell even pointed out in the article that the Petersburg contingent arrived late, at 11:00 a.m., which delayed the parade's start, although he did observe that they were given lunch at the Armory.[29]

Many other groups participated on this and other such occasions. Mitchell mentioned, for instance, a "Negro Insurance Society, Rev. W.W. Browne, founder," and a "band

Editor John Mitchell Jr. in full-dress Knights of Pythias uniform, circa 1895. *John Thomas Mitchell family collection.*

from the Va. Normal and Collegiate Institute" that "discourses excellent music." In addition, youth groups participated. Mitchell mentioned one, the "Peterson's Zouaves, a body of little boys attired in suits in keeping with their names." Banners also featured prominently in the parade, some sporting such historical or political mottoes as "In 1860 slaves; in 1890 bankers" and "Vote the Dollar Ballot."[30]

A second article, published eight years later, reported on a January 1898 parade and celebrations of Lincoln's January 1, 1863 official announcement of the Emancipation Proclamation. Its timing was interesting for another reason. The *Planet* published this article just one month before hostilities precipitating the Spanish-American War broke out, a war that would within a year bring to an end the black militia units in Virginia.

As before, Mitchell featured the involvement of both militia companies and fraternal orders, especially the Knights of Pythias. Many editions of the *Planet* reported information on the Knights of Pythias, mostly announcements of meetings and decisions but also significant activities and developments. In this article, the *Planet* editor reminded his readers of his high rank within the Pythians by referencing his full title, "Brigadier General of the Knights of Pythias, N.A., S.A.E., A., A. and A." And, as before, he referred to himself as the "Chief Marshal" for the parade. He obviously was a very prominent figure in the community.[31]

This article also illustrates the Armory's central place in the community's celebrations. Note, interestingly, the mention of the Battalion Band:

Etching of Company C militia member in his "magnificent blue full dress uniform." *Richmond Planet*, April 10, 1897. *Library of Virginia*.

> *The Y.M.C.A. Building, 214 East Leigh Street, was the scene of the busiest activity. Here was located the headquarters of the Chief Marshal, John Mitchell, Jr.*
>
> *The First Battalion Band repaired to the armory where the state troops were in waiting and a few moments later, the sound of martial music was heard and the splendidly equipped force headed by the Major's Staff…put in an appearance.*[32]

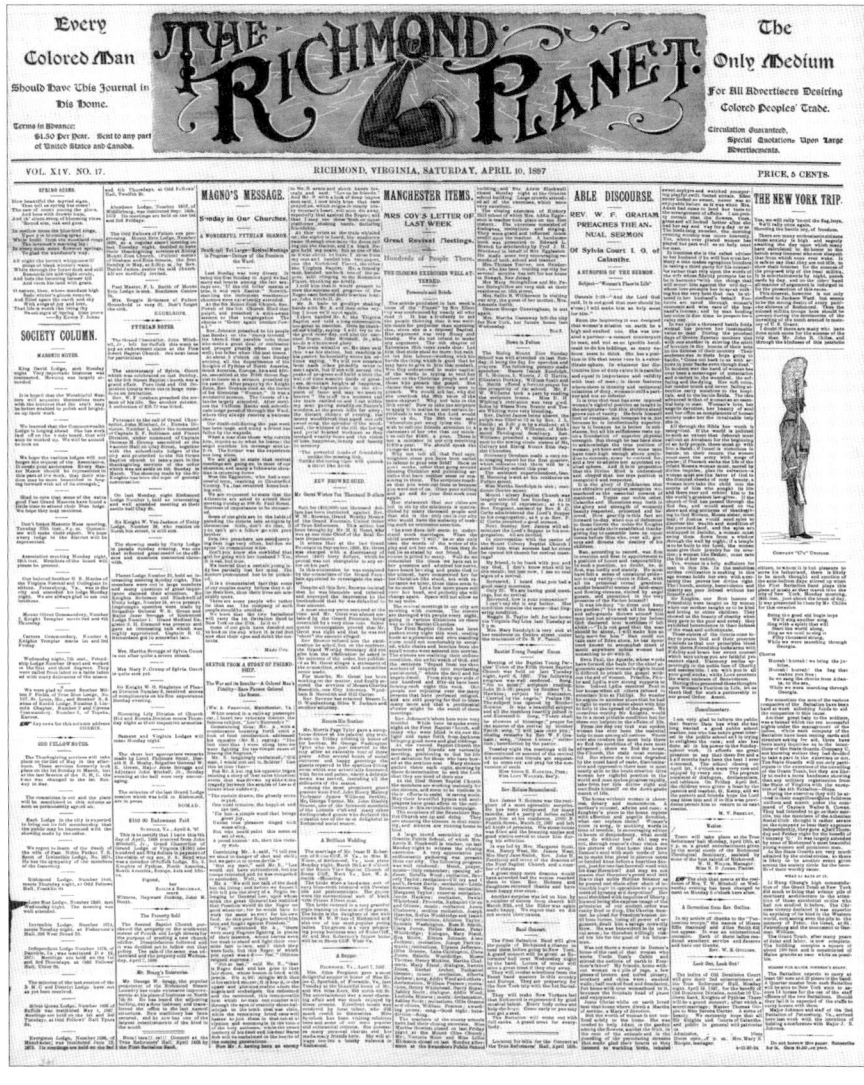

As with other reports on such celebrations, this one also focused on the pomp and ceremony—especially the "brilliantly attired" outfits, mounted horses, disciplined soldiers and the Pythian Band:

> *It was 1:50 P.M., when the line moved. John Mitchell, Jr., Brigadier General of the Knights of Pythias, N.A., S.A.E., A., A. and A., and Chief Marshal led the way, followed by his brilliantly attired and mounted staff. As they passed in review, the state militia had the customary honors,*

> and the Uniform Rank of the K. of P. was not slow to follow....Colonels Mitchell, Chiles and Johnson wore chapeaux.
>
> The glittering heavily gold plated uniform presented a rich, magnificent appearance. It consisted of the silk folding K. of P. chapeaux gold cord shoulder-knots, gold-cord aiguillette, gold plated belt and sword, gauntlets and the dark blue regulation suits as per regulation, ornamented with gold plated buttons....The Brigadier General wore the silk-folding chapeau, K. of P. Regulations, heavily gold plated epaulets, gold plated belt and sword, a 14-foot long, imported silk sash, as per regulations, gauntlets and a suit of dark blue cloth.
>
> As these Pythian officers moved up Leigh Street, there was a shout of surprise. The Battalion wheeled into line and the Pythian Band played a patriotic air.
>
> The K. of P. Battalion, Uniform Rank, was under the command of Capt. Thomas M. Crump, Eureka Company, Number 1, commanded by Capt. R.S. Nelson and Planet Company. Number 8 by Lieut J.A. Smith.
>
> The Marshals presented a handsome appearance wearing sashes of navy blue and being mounted. They took place at the head of the subordinate department of the Pythians, which presented a fine appearance with their handsome badges.[33]

Other orders participated in the parade as well. "The Knights of Damon were represented by two mounted officers. The Order of Love and Charity had many carriages in which were seated the female members of that organization."[34]

The article included one interesting side note about Mitchell's younger and only sibling, Thomas W. Mitchell, who also held high rank in the Knights of Pythias. Thomas apparently fell from his horse along the parade route. But, as the article points out, he got up and, securing another, went on his way:

> At the corner of First and Leigh streets, the horse of Adjutant General Thomas W. Mitchell became unmanageable and fell to the ground and that officer narrowly escaped being caught under him. He however took his place in line, and on Main [S]treet another horse was sent him and he took his place among his fellow members of the staff at the head of the column.[35]

The parade culminated at the First African Baptist Church, which sat on the corner of Fourteenth and Broad Streets. However, with the building filled to capacity, the First Battalion decided to march back to its armory. First African Baptist occupies a long and historically prominent position within Richmond's African American community. So it was not incidental that this parade began at the Leigh Street Armory and ended at the First African Baptist Church, a distance of approximately one and a half miles.[36]

This third article is notable because of the incongruity of where the black troops drilled in Richmond—around the Lee statue on Monument Avenue—and also because of its timing. The *Planet* published it just before the troops left for camp to train for the Spanish-American War. This event thus occurred while recruitment for the war was well underway, a time, in other words, when those volunteering to serve (and their families and friends) were filled with high patriotic fervor.

When the soldiers reached the monument to Robert E. Lee, the article read—dripping with irony and understatement—the battalion was not intimidated by the specter of the iconic structure, presenting the public with a most engaging performance:

> *The First Battalion, Virginia Volunteer Infantry celebrated its 2nd Anniversary Thursday, June 16, 1898 by a street parade, battalion drill and banquet at the handsome armory.*
>
> *At about 4:30 P.M., the men filed out while the band stationed at Price and Leigh Sts., discoursed lively airs.*
>
> *The stentorian voice of the soldierly major was heard and he proceeded to the head of the column.... The line of march was to 7th St, to Broad to Adam, to Grace to the Baptist College to Lee Monument. Here a most imposing sight was witnessed. A battalion drill with its picturesque surroundings was a treat in store for the sightseeing population.*[37]

The "stentorian voice" that came through loud and clear, as if the voice of many men rather than one, was that of Battalion Commander Major J.B. Johnson.

CHAPTER 2

# THE ARMORIES

## America's Nineteenth-Century Castles

That imposing two-story brick structure on Leigh Street in Richmond, Virginia, is just one of hundreds of armories that many American cities built in a veritable explosion of armory construction that spanned more than thirty years, beginning in the late 1870s and ending roughly in 1915. Some of these were relatively modest in their furnishings and décor; many others were more opulent and impressive.

The State of New York alone built more than eighty armories, some of which would become national models for armory construction. New York City, for example, built its massive Seventh Regiment Armory in 1880 at the astonishing cost of approximately $600,000. This stands in stark contrast with the $10,000 the City of Richmond spent on the Leigh Street Armory fifteen years later. Since New York built that armory very early in the late nineteenth-century period of armory construction, the Seventh Regiment emerged as a compelling example of armory design that many other cities would emulate. A grand and treasured building, the Seventh still stands on Park Avenue, now serving as a recognized tourist destination and center for the arts.[38]

The nineteenth-century wave of armory construction coincided with a national shift in architectural preference favoring functionalism over the heretofore-popular Greek Revival style. Architects in those days argued that buildings should resemble the purposes for which they were designed and the ideals to which they appealed. As armory historian Roger M. Fogelson explains, cities built armories that would reflect their military character,

New York's Seventh Regiment Armory, photo taken 1984. *Library of Congress.*

command a sense of authority, represent the power of the state, epitomize order and stand ready for action.[39]

Image thus eclipsed functionality in those late nineteenth-century castles, as their designers added thick foundations and walls, narrow windows, broad entryways and tall, crenellated turrets and rooflines to convey power and order. Historically, such features were essential to defend against attack. The crenellations—the squared and sequenced gaps at the tops of rooflines—protected warriors against incoming arrows, bullets and other projectiles. As the stratagems and technologies of war changed over time, such features evolved into prized architectural flourishes and ornamentations. This was especially true for the late nineteenth-century armories that functioned more as training and meeting centers and leadership headquarters than battle-hardened centers for defense. Armories also served as launching points for parades and, less frequently, for initiating defensive maneuvers on city streets in response to the occasional civil disruption that any one city might experience. In other words, the overall mass, stylized battlements and the expense of these structures bore little relationship to the purposes for which the cities built them.

Postcard showing three Richmond armories, circa 1915. *Virginia Commonwealth University*.

The Richmond Light Infantry Blues Armory, built in 1910. *Virginia Commonwealth University*.

Richmond rebuilt the old Regimental Infantry (Greys) in 1913. *Library of Virginia.*

Richmond erected five different armories. It built the first, the Regimental Infantry (or Greys) Armory, very early in the period of armory construction, in 1882. The high-water mark of armory construction in Richmond, however, was 1895. In that year, the city built three such structures: the Leigh Street Armory, the Richmond Howitzers Armory and the First Regimental Cavalry Armory. Fifteen years later, after the turn of the century, Richmond built the Blues Armory in 1910. In 1913, Richmond officials had the Greys Armory demolished and constructed a replacement the next year. Only two of the five armories are still standing: the Leigh Street and the Blues. Leigh Street currently serves as the home of Richmond's Black History Museum and Cultural Center of Virginia. As of this date, the city is still searching for a purpose and economic rationale to support restoration of the Blues Armory.

## The Armories of the Gilded Age

These grand armories were very much products and reflections of the Gilded Age. Mark Twain and Charles Dudley Warner coined this term in the latter nineteenth century to reflect a preference the wealthy elite had for ostentatious styles of living. Their buildings were often gaudy and excessive, reflecting unmistakably their owners' perceived self-importance and unprecedented personal wealth. In this period, a clique of prominent, powerful and often young elites—Rockefeller, Morgan, Carnegie, Mellon, Vanderbilt, Astor and others—accumulated an outlandishly disproportionate percentage of the nation's wealth. They lived impressive and highly visible lives and, in the process, left behind financial and structural legacies so significant that their names' currency continues.[40]

A number of societal and economic changes contributed directly to the period's eruption in armory construction. The rapid evolution in key technologies, the emergence of new and powerful industries and the monopolization of vital markets—such as oil, steel, rail, finance, coal, shipping, retail, barbed wire and hotels—all opened up new opportunities for economic and societal advance. At the same time, these factors exacerbated economic disparities and generated disruptive market forces that dramatically altered the nature of work. Most especially, they amplified the power employers could exert over laborers in the workplace.[41]

Those history-changing economic developments had a darker side as well. The so-called robber barons, perched at the top of the economic ladder, often demonstrated little concern for the welfare of their workers and, more generally, for the poor. Their unchecked economic and political power and their capriciousness in business decision-making greatly unsettled workers, leading many to form unions that then organized strikes and engaged in what turned out to be highly disruptive forms of civil disobedience.[42]

At the same time, immigrants flooded into the country, including some believed to be communists, anarchists or, simply, extremists. The fear of outsiders contributed to a growing anxiety among many workers over the prospect of losing their jobs. Feelings of alienation and a sense of having lost control spread over a country changing far too rapidly. Such conditions contributed to unpredictable swings in the economy and, in their wake, widespread social upheavals that often spawned violence and the destruction of property. Some of this was so extensive that historians have referred to this period as "the great upheaval" to reflect the scale and impacts the disorder created.[43]

*Right*: Mark Twain, 1902. *Library of Congress.*

*Below*: The southwest flank of the Vanderbilts' Breakers house, Newport, Rhode Island. *Library of Congress.*

# Richmond's Leigh Street Armory & African American Militia

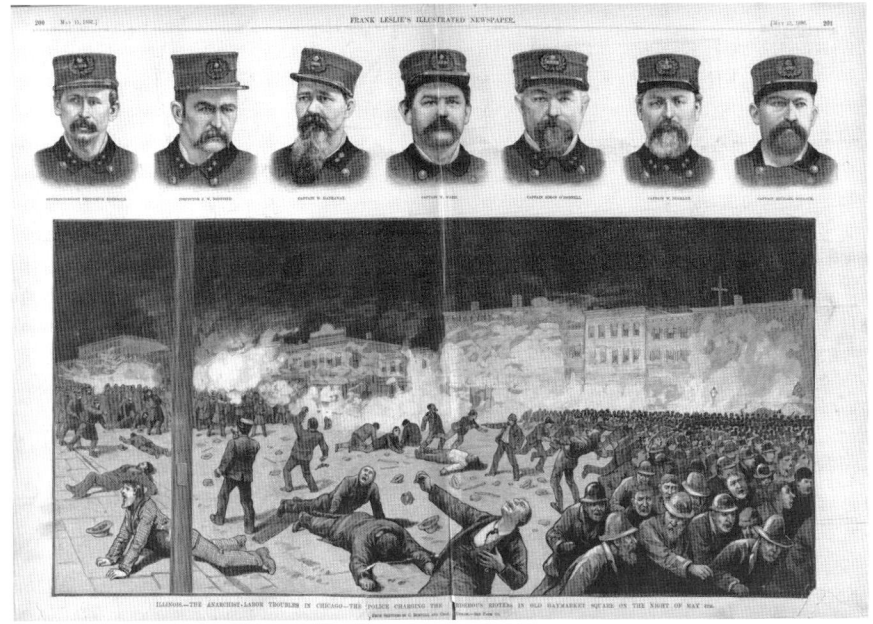

*Above*: Chicago Haymarket Affair, May 1886. *Library of Congress*.

*Opposite*: Robber barons as Robin Hood—depicts such financial giants as William H. Vanderbilt, Cyrus W. Field and others robbing a "taxpayer," 1886, *Library of Congress*.

Unfortunately, the country did not address the long-term inequities that drove the civil disturbances in the first place. Instead, fear and demagoguery focused the nation's attention on the use of force to stem the spreading violence. The remarkable Haymarket Affair, an event that derives its name from Chicago's Haymarket Square, is a prime example of this pattern of response. In May 1886, a demonstration at the square initially began peacefully as strikers demanded eight-hour workdays. The relative calm did not last long, however. On the first day, police killed several workers, and the second day was even more dramatic. Someone tossed a bomb into the crowd, killing police officers and eliciting a fierce gun battle that left many dead and wounded. While other important confrontations occurred in that period, this one alone impacted labor relations not only in Chicago but in the United States as a whole.[44]

Cities and states responded by focusing on defense and order. They turned first to their local police for help, but unfortunately, their numbers were too few and they were untrained and ill equipped to deal with unwieldy social disruptions, as the Haymarket Affair demonstrated so vividly. Municipalities also considered the United States Army to be a viable option. This, too, produced insufficient numbers and was costly to use in this way. They mostly relied on their militias for defense, the ranks of which the Civil War had greatly depleted. So they built up their forces, and the numbers of militiamen grew rapidly, reaching over 100,000 by the 1890s.[45]

In return, militia leaders argued persuasively that they needed armories in which to meet, train and prepare for emergencies. They also wanted them to be so constructed that they would easily provide secure defense in case of attack. It was true that striking workers, if not properly controlled, could inflict considerable damage to property and even threaten lives. But these were not heavily weaponized invading forces from overseas. They were strikers and rioters who were ill matched against the well-trained and armed militia units. The threat they posed could hardly justify the major investments in costly fortifications those armories provided. Reflecting Gilded Age excess, those massive armories were thus very much over the top. They were large and expensive, vastly over fortified and, as it turned out, built to protect against a relatively impotent, poorly organized and temporary threat.[46]

The Armory, University of Minnesota, Minneapolis, Minnesota, circa 1905. *Library of Congress.*

Cadet Armory, New York, circa 1904. *Library of Congress.*

It is important to understand that post–Civil War armories differed markedly from those the military built prior to the war. Unlike their earlier counterparts, they were not warehouses for armaments, nor were they dusty centers for the manufacture of weapons. Rather, they were comfortable and grand places where the militia companies, battalions and regiments could meet and train. They were also often the center places for community celebrations and revelry, greatly amplified by the pageantry of soldiers, bedecked with sabers and sashes, marching in city streets on foot or on horseback to the reverberations of military bands. Notably, the cities did not build their armories along their borders for defensive purposes or next to rivers to facilitate the shipping of armaments. Because militiamen wanted armories to be accessible to their homes, some cities even built them in the most prominent sections of town.

Because they were so sturdily built and, in many cases, are such striking examples of the Gilded Age today, many armories continue on, not as military garrisons, but as the protected remnants of a highly consequential

# Richmond's Leigh Street Armory & African American Militia

*Above*: State Armory of Lowell, Massachusetts, between 1900 and 1910. *Library of Congress*.

*Left*: Cadet Armory, Boston, Massachusetts, circa 1904. *Library of Congress*.

Holyoke, Massachusetts Armory, between 1900 and 1910. *Library of Congress.*

period in the nation's history. Most of these are now hotels, large gymnasiums, museums and other public and private places. The surviving armories thus stand today as silent and outsized sentinels reminding us of how fear drove the nation to react defensively, rather than address directly the underlying inequities structured around race and class.

## The Irony of a Black Armory in Richmond

Against the backdrop of New York and other cities that built armories is one little-known, but important, fact: Richmond, Virginia, is the only American city to have built an armory for a black militia. Many cities provided their black troops access to armories, but these were rented halls or other facilities. They were not free-standing buildings constructed expressly for the use of black soldiers, as was the Leigh Street Armory.

This is especially important, as those large, imposing buildings were costly. Their construction burdened city budgets already constrained by the demands for schools, roads and the like. Thus, to build an armory for an African American militia group was especially problematic, as this constituted a major departure from established racial norms at that time. Perhaps more importantly, it represented a tacit enhancement of the African American soldier's position within the delicately balanced militia structures that the states and cities had established following the Civil War.

More importantly, this occurred in Richmond, Virginia, arguably the most unlikely setting in which a major break with racial traditions would have occurred. The significance of the Leigh Street Armory's construction is thus not its physical features, size, architectural beauty or the lavishness of its appointments. In fact, it was a relatively modest version of the armories of the day. Rather, therefore, it is the improbability of it having been built at all. More especially, it is that Richmond, Virginia, the very epicenter of early African American history, would have been the only city in this country to erect an armory for a black militia battalion.

Possibly even most importantly, Richmond built the Armory in 1895, just as Jim Crow was being legally sanctioned across the country. Seven years later, in 1902, Virginia rewrote its state constitution, formalizing a pattern of discrimination that was by then well underway. Many other southern states did the same, setting forth in explicit language a legal structure that severely restricted the rights of African Americans for decades. Thus, while the timing of the Armory's construction is noteworthy, more telling is the city and state that built it.

It is well known that Virginia played an overwhelmingly important role in American history generally. It is widely acknowledged that Britain established its first permanent North American community as Jamestown, Virginia, in 1607. In the decades preceding 1776, Virginia was the most populous and

Thomas Rice, wearing the costume of his character, "Jim Crow," circa 1835. *Library of Congress.*

possibly most influential of the thirteen colonies. Prominent Virginians—like George Washington, Thomas Jefferson, James Madison, George Mason and Patrick Henry—played leading roles in drafting the country's foundational documents, including the Declaration of Independence, the Constitution and the Bill of Rights. Even Richmond native John Marshall played an essential role in the nation's founding. As the country's fourth chief justice of the Supreme Court and longest to serve on the court, Marshall almost single-handedly sorted out in precedent-setting decisions the relative powers of the three branches of United States government.[47]

Much less appreciated is Virginia's central place in early African American history. In 1619, the first documented Africans set foot on British North American soil less than one hundred miles from Richmond, at Point Comfort (Fort Monroe). From that point on, Virginia steadily moved toward codifying racial slavery. In every federal census from 1790 to 1860, Virginia retained its position as the state with the highest enslaved population. Virginia was key to American slavery in other crucial ways as well. Most especially, prominent Virginians played pivotal roles in writing a constitution that effectively provided a framework that maintained the right to own property—including human chattel—as sacred, defendable and quintessentially American.[48]

First Africans arrive in Virginia. Published in *Harper's Weekly*, 1619. *Library of Congress.*

After 1808, economic changes allowed Virginia to emerge as a leader in the domestic slave trade, a position it would sustain until the end of the Civil War. The growing of tobacco gradually shifted to the Deep South, which left Virginia with a significant oversupply of the enslaved. The invention of the cotton gin, the Louisiana Purchase and other economic changes further stimulated a rapidly growing demand for cheap labor in the South and West. As a consequence, Virginia's enslaved became an important source of new revenue for the owners and dealers in human chattel. Virginia's numerous slave traders broke up families, sold individuals in the burgeoning numbers of auction houses and on outdoor

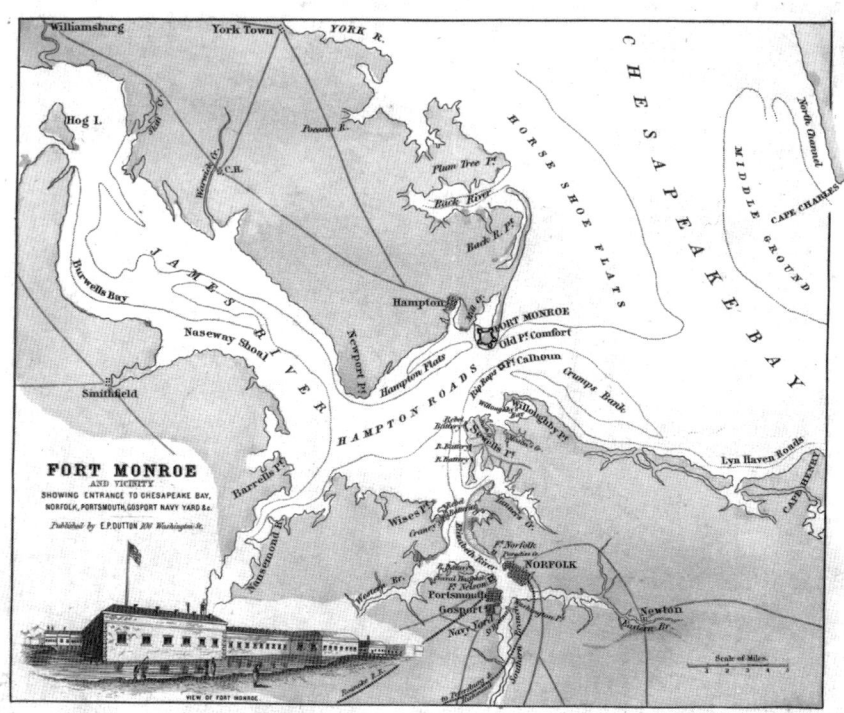

Map showing Fort Monroe ("Old Pt. Comfort") at entrance to Chesapeake Bay, circa 186-. *Library of Congress.*

auction blocks and then transported their chattel property by ship, train or in slave coffles over land to ports and other markets across the South and West, including New Orleans, Savannah and Nashville.[49]

Richmond itself was at the center of this odious business. Its slave markets thrived in the Shockoe Bottom, located very near Virginia's symbol of freedom, the capitol that Thomas Jefferson designed. While Richmond became the second-largest slave-trading center nationally (New Orleans was number one overall), it was the undisputed lead "wholesaler" of enslaved persons in the nation.

During the Civil War, Virginia, and Richmond especially, was central to the secessionist fight to preserve states' rights to enslave. Richmond served as the capital of the Confederate States of America, and the state produced a number of the important Confederate generals and other officers. The warring parties of the Union and Confederacy fought key battles throughout Virginia, including the consequential clashes that forced the

Alexandria slave pen, circa 1861–65. *Library of Congress.*

"Moving day at Richmond," the end of the Confederacy. *Library of Congress.*

collapse of the Confederate government in Richmond and Lee's surrender at Appomattox.[50]

The foregoing, together, make Richmond's decision to construct an armory for its black soldiers so very implausible. It would have been predictable had Richmond in that period erected a large, well-appointed school building for black students or invested more heavily in utility infrastructure or community beautification projects in black neighborhoods, comparable to those provided in white communities. Instead, officials built an impressive military fortress for its black militia battalion in the very heart of the city. Adding to the implausibility, black soldiers training in local rented facilities and marching with weapons in the city's streets were threatening enough to white sensitivities. Now, in the wake of the Leigh Street Armory's construction, those same soldiers filed out of an impressive and expensive building that tax dollars, mostly of white citizens, had funded. From the Armory's broad front doors and granite steps, the black officers mounted grand steeds, while others marched in polished boots. They all expressed, with pride of accomplishment and embodiment of masculinity unavailable to other black soldiers across the country, a belief that full equality was nearing.

The Leigh Street Armory thus stands as one of Virginia's most iconic and ironic physical symbols of America's long and difficult experiment with race and the struggle over basic civil and human rights. It also serves as an emblem for the expectations and striving of Virginia's African Americans in that narrow but fleeting window of hope between the end of the Civil War and the full unmasking of racial segregation in this country.

## Laying the Predicate for the Armory's Construction

As might be expected, the distinctiveness of the Armory's construction did not go unnoticed or unappreciated by Richmond's African American community. John Mitchell Jr., the prominent editor of the *Richmond Planet* and a key figure in getting city officials to build the Armory, was himself well aware of the building's uniqueness. In his summary on the history following the opening of the Armory, he began his narrative by saying, "Richmond is the only city in this country, so far as we have been advised, which has provided so well for its colored citizen soldiery as to erect an

The *Richmond Planet* masthead, December 21, 1895. *Library of Virginia.*

armory building."[51] Mitchell knew then what history has since revealed—that that very special structure was the only one of its kind. The conditions necessary for the Armory's construction were present in Richmond at just the right time. Six conditions, in particular, should be highlighted.

First, Virginia's African American militia men worked very hard from 1872 to 1899 to gain the respect of leading figures in the community. Federal statutes had forced Virginia and other southern states to allow black citizens to volunteer to serve in their militia forces. And in response, black Virginians rushed to sign up, producing one of the largest contingents of black militiamen across the country. As trailblazers in a highly racialized environment, they were fully cognizant that they needed to act unswervingly in the city and state's interests and to remain nonpartisan and noncontroversial. The evidence suggests that the black soldiers conformed well to community expectations. This is notable, considering Virginia's history with slavery and the continuing and growing racial divide in the state and nation.[52]

This is also notable because, like most southern states, Virginia provided limited and unequal levels of resources to the black militia troops, as compared to that which it apportioned to their white counterparts. Many of Virginia's black troops, for example, lacked regulation uniforms, updated weapons, appropriate munitions and adequate training. Still, the troops appear not to have challenged the authorities too assertively over the obvious inequities.[53]

It is thus likely that the troops' compliance with expectations contributed to state leaders' willingness to activate on at least five occasions (discussed earlier) black troops from Richmond and other locations to deal with state crises. While government leaders constrained the black soldiers' involvement in all such situations, the militia companies appear to have performed their duties with dignity and decorum, earning plaudits for their efforts. The black soldiers also won favor by marching in their city streets, leading emancipation and other parades, participating in the inaugurations of governors and U.S. presidents and competing with white militia troops in Washington, D.C. After the construction of the Armory, they even marched in a New York

City parade to celebrate completion of President Grant's tomb.[54] The point is that the black militia members behaved as exemplary citizens up to the time Richmond built the Armory. This is not to say that there were no controversies in those years. There were. Racial tensions across the state rose steadily from the beginning when blacks first joined the Virginia Volunteers in 1872.

This leads to a second, closely related reason why Richmond might have agreed to build the Armory. In the Reconstruction era, southern governors formed so-called negro militias to protect against violence that disgruntled ex-Confederates increasingly perpetrated against their governments and the newly freed African Americans. From 1866 to 1871, Congress passed various acts that supported the governors in this effort. Importantly, those acts sought to protect a broad range of rights for black citizens, including, of particular interest to this history, the right to bear arms. Because it opted for a compromise government rather than one controlled by radical Republicans, Virginia was one of two southern states that did not form African American militias in those unsettled few years immediately following the Civil War.[55] This decision undoubtedly contributed to a relatively more receptive climate when it came time for the state to admit black militia companies into the Virginia Volunteers in 1872 and, just over two decades later, for Richmond to construct the Leigh Street Armory in 1895.

While the foregoing two conditions provide context, they do not explain why Richmond specifically voted in 1894 to provide $10,000 to construct the Armory. The next four factors help to explain how this happened and why it happened at that particular point in time.

A third contributing factor was the assertive initiative the First Battalion's leadership provided. Virginia designated Richmond's contingent of black militia members as the First Battalion Virginia Volunteers. Major Joseph B. Johnson, the battalion's commanding officer at the time, led the effort. In 1884, Johnson persuaded the city to acquire land for a black armory. His persistent efforts culminated in the city's decision in 1888 to acquire the site at the corner of Leigh and St. Peter Streets where the Armory now stands. He also played a key role in persuading Richmond to fund the Armory's construction.[56]

A fourth factor was the role Jackson Ward politicians played in Richmond government. Shortly after the Civil War, Richmond formed the segregated and gerrymandered Jackson Ward, within which the city's black citizens were able, for a finite period of time, to elect black representatives to the city council. In the year preceding construction of the Armory, for instance,

Jackson Ward voters elected eight representatives to the city council, placing members on both the board of aldermen and the common council. This represented one-sixth of the council's total membership of forty-eight. Six of the eight were black, two were white.[57] Thus, while Richmond's black community had limited real power, it did have a voice at a critical time. This provided an essential forum within which to work the political structure and, as it happened, to prevail upon city council members to fund construction of a black armory.

A fifth condition needed to be present for Richmond to have built the Armory was the leadership provided by a specific city council member, Alderman John Mitchell Jr. Mitchell was also editor of the politically important *Richmond Planet*, a locally and nationally prominent black newspaper at that time. His paper gave him a loud megaphone that, in combination with his considerable political skills and stature, he used effectively to influence city council deliberations. This was at a time when the Armory's funding literally hung in the balance.

Finally, Colonel W.E. Cutshaw, a prominent and highly respected figure in Richmond at large and within the Richmond city administration, provided informed and fair-minded support for building the Leigh Street Armory. Having served for some time as the city engineer, Cutshaw advised lawmakers at crucially important points regarding engineering, financial and design issues pertaining to the Armory's construction. He was widely respected within the community for his many contributions to the city's environment, especially to key public buildings, city streets, sidewalks, schools and, of course, armories. He not only supported the acquisition of land for the Armory but also offered timely advice when city council debated construction funding. And notably, his office drew up the architectural plans from which the city built the Armory.[58] A respected member of the white community—and, interestingly, a prominent former Confederate officer—Cutshaw's careful reasoning most certainly helped city leaders overcome an inherent aversion to investing in the black community, most especially in an expensive building that black militia volunteers would use.

All of these factors, together, contributed to the officials' decision to build the Leigh Street Armory. But the leadership that John Mitchell Jr., Jackson Ward council members, Colonel Cutshaw and the officers of Richmond's black militia provided undoubtedly made all the difference. Without their persistent efforts, that unique facility surely would never have become a reality.

CHAPTER 3

# THE IMPROBABLE
# LEIGH STREET ARMORY

*Jackson Ward, City Politics and a Fighting Editor*

In 1884, the First Battalion was effectively homeless. Even though the Volunteers did have a facility to use for their purposes, it was far from adequate and not their own. The process leading to building the Leigh Street Armory began in 1884 when Richmond city officials authorized $4,000 to acquire the necessary land. Funding for the actual construction came ten years later.

*Richmond Planet* editor John Mitchell Jr. described the facility they were using at that time: "[T]he Battalion was meeting in a hall in an alley which hall was not large enough for one company. Peace and harmony having prevailed, the question of more commodious quarters arose. The old Union Hotel on 7th St., was secured which after some use was found unsafe for Armory purposes."[59]

Something had to be done to secure a new facility for the battalion, and the still fluid race relations helped make this possible. Rather than rent yet another, likely inadequate facility in the city, Richmond officials decided to build an armory for the First Battalion. Once the city agreed to acquire a site, the battalion commander, Major Johnson, and his officers began the process of searching for suitable options.[60]

Mitchell wrote in his newspaper:

> In 1884 the city purchased the site on St. Peter and Leigh streets at the cost of $4,000.00. He [battalion commander Major Johnson] then appointed a committee consisting of the captains of the companies,

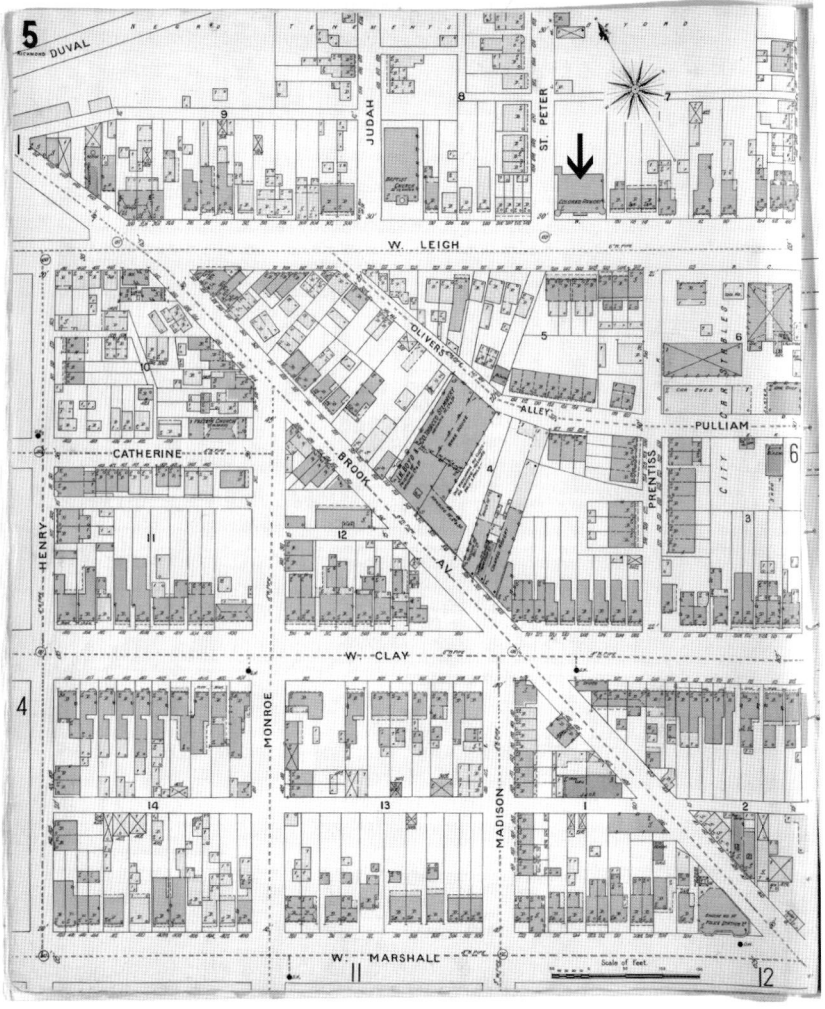

The old Armory (listed as "Colored Armory") on the 1895 Sanborn map. *Library of Virginia.*

*looking to the erection of an armory thereon. This committee prosecuted its work until 1893 without any apparent success. In November 1893 this committee was relieved of its duty by the Major, who took the matter in his own hands assisted by Capt. S.H. Dismond, Lieut. W. Issac Johnson and Hon[.] John Mitchell, Jr., who worked indefatigably for 12 months and one week up to the time of the appropriation from the city of $10,000.*[61]

Mitchell thus credited Major Johnson and his officers for having convinced the city to appropriate monies for the land. Mitchell said of their work, "This effort on the part of these gentlemen, who did so much work in urging and securing the liberal appropriations through the City Council and the subsequent erection of this magnificent structure as the armory of the First Battalion is a monument of honor, to all who had a part in securing it, for the purposes for which it was built."[62] After the city approved the search for land in 1884, the focus shifted to finding a suitable site and then to persuading the city to fund the Armory's construction—tasks that together took a decade to complete.

Despite his detailing of the aforementioned events, Mitchell did make one error in his summary of the history surrounding the Armory's construction. His statement concerning the city's 1884 purchase of the site at St. Peter and Leigh was incorrect. In 1884, the city approved funding to acquire land, but it took another four years to select an actual, specific property. Reports in Richmond's *Daily Times* indicate that in 1886, the militia expressed its desire that the city not limit itself to Jackson Ward when considering the site of the Armory. However, by January 1888, the city had seemingly narrowed its choices to two Jackson Ward sites, one at Leigh and Third Streets and another nearby on Third between Leigh and Jackson Streets. By the end of January 1888, city council's committee recommended purchasing land, 62½ feet front by 120 feet deep, on the corner of Leigh and St. Peter Streets, and in May 1888, Richmond City Council decided to allocate $4,000 to purchase the land to build the Armory.[63]

## Securing Funding for Construction

In the midst of the search for land, city council gave considerable thought to the Armory's construction. After consultation with City Engineer Colonel Cutshaw, the committee requested input from the battalion as to their building needs so as to determine the cost of the building. By September 1888, four months after the decision was made to purchase the specific parcel of land, city council considered a resolution to appropriate $20,000 for the armory building. In December 1887, Colonel Cutshaw had already proposed a still higher amount for construction—about $25,000 or $35,000—in addition to alternate sites on Sixth and Seventh Streets. The city took no action on that proposal.[64] The details on Cutshaw's initial role in erecting an armory provide additional evidence of the city engineer's constructive and assertive support for the black militia soldiers. Importantly, he continued to support construction of the Armory, from the decision to buy the land through to the time the city approved monies for its construction.

Yet by May 1893, Richmond City Council's two chambers, Alderman and Common Council, lacked the votes needed to proceed with construction. Persistence on the part of the Armory's promoters, nevertheless, eventually paid off. Timing was everything in this. It did not hurt that Richmond had already constructed a white armory—the Regimental (or Richmond Greys) Armory—eleven years earlier, in 1882. And it was planning to build two more—the Howitzers and the Cavalry—the same year the Leigh Street Armory was being considered. Those pushing for the Leigh Street Armory were thus able to apply a fairness argument to pressure city council to vote yes on the Armory's construction, a point John Mitchell Jr. made in his 1894 description of the process leading to a final funding decision.

In January 1894, city council finally voted to fund the building, approving $7,500, which was far less than the amounts first considered. Mitchell also noted a favorable decision to appropriate $25,000 for another armory, "the Richmond Howizters, white."[65] Although there was a dramatic lack of parity between funding for the Leigh Street Armory and other peer institutions, Mitchell's recording of the historic document, to which Richmond Mayor J. Taylor Ellyson affixed his signature in January 1894, is noteworthy:

> *Be it resolved by the Council of the city of Richmond, the Common Council, concurring that the Auditor of the city, be and is hereby authorized to issue $7,500 in 4 per cent bonds of the City of Richmond in the form prescribed by the Ordinance on the subject on the demand of the Finance Committee; and the said committee is empowered to dispose of the same in such manner and at such times as they may deem best for the interest of the city, and the net proceeds of said bonds shall be placed to the credit of an account known as the Armory for the First Battalion, Va.*
>
> *Volunteer Infantry to be drawn on by Warrants approved by the committee on Grounds and Buildings after such warrants shall have been signed by the City Engineer and offered to be paid by said committee on Grounds and Buildings.*
>
> *Adopted by the Board of Aldermen, May 8th 1893, Ayes, 16; Noes 1. Concurred in by the Common Council January 1st, 1894. Ayes, 20; Noes, 0.*[66]

In July 1894, before all bids had come in, Mitchell expressed hope that the Armory would have a drill shed, as did most armories of that era. He wrote, optimistically, "Should the appropriation of $7,500 be sufficient, a drill shed will be erected over the yard under which the militia can drill in rainy weather."[72] But it quickly became obvious not only that residual monies would not be available for the shed but also that the approved amount would be insufficient to cover construction costs for the Armory itself.

Colonel Cutshaw proposed adding $2,500 to the original amount, bringing the total to $10,000. The council supported his proposal and sent a bill approving supplementary funding to the new mayor, Richard M. Taylor. This was a key moment in this process, as Mayor Taylor had only a few months earlier, as a member of the board of aldermen, voted angrily against funding the Armory. He promptly vetoed the bill approving the supplementary funds and sent it back to the council with the following comment explaining his reasons for doing so:

> *I return the resolution, adopted by the Board of Aldermen September 11, 1894, and concurred in by the Common Council, October 1, 1894, appropriating $2,500 for armory for First Battalion, Virginia volunteers, infantry, without my approval, as I deem it unnecessary, unwise, and against public policy to maintain colored soldiers in this city, and this battalion is composed of colored soldiers.*[73]

Mayor Taylor left no doubt that his position on the Armory had not changed. His reasons made a dramatic statement opposing the threatening specter of black soldiers—a telling read of the intersection between blackness and masculinity.

The *Alexandria Gazette*, and surely other white newspapers in the region, not only supported the mayor's decision but agreed with his reasons. The *Gazette* wrote:

> *Mayor Taylor of Richmond, vetoed a bill increasing by $2,500 an appropriation for a [N]egro armory in that city, for the wise and sufficient reason that where there are so many negroes, "it is against public policy to maintain military organizations composed entirely of that race." The Board of Alderman, however, passed the bill over his veto. But, as the* Gazette *implied, it is not what Richmond does, but what it does not that may be most surprising.*[74]

The board of aldermen then debated whether council should override the mayor's veto. In covering the debate, Mitchell referenced a number of the arguments an Alderman Blake, who, interestingly, was not in the Jackson Ward contingent, made in favor of override. First, Blake pointed to the annual expense of $500 that the city was paying to rent the space the battalion currently used for its armory. He also stressed the location's inadequacy as being unfit for its designated purpose. And he argued that since the Committee on Finance and both branches of the council had heretofore supported funding for construction, it should override the mayor's veto.[75]

Mitchell then reported on some of the key points he himself had made in the debate, including what he perceived to be the central issue from the community perspective—the need for there to be "colored troops" in Richmond: "The battalion was here for the protection of the lives and property of the citizens," Mitchell reasoned. "He [Alderman Blake] would not enter into discussion of the wisdom of having colored troops; the fact was plain that they were here to stay." The debate being completed, Mitchell reported, Alderman Blake moved that the board approve the additional funding. It did, with a unanimous vote of fourteen ayes and zero noes.[76] It is truly remarkable, given the times, that Richmond's white-dominated city

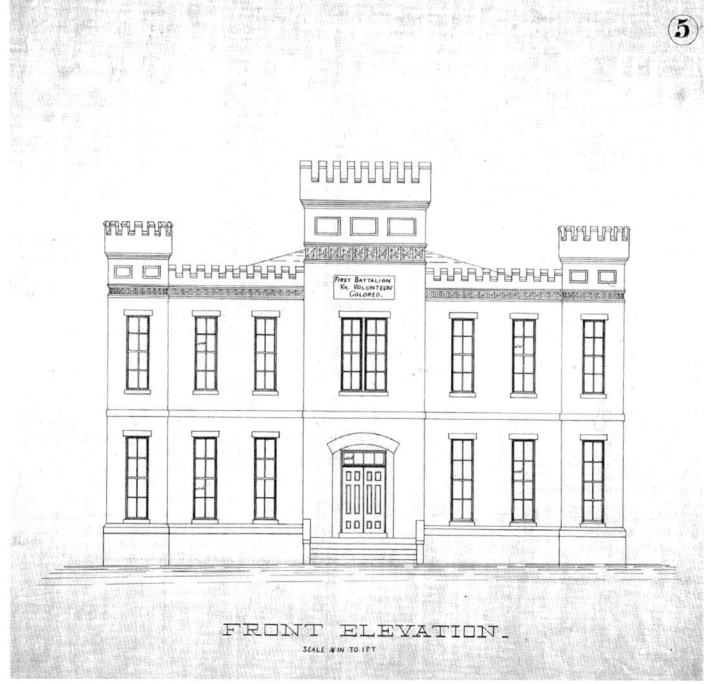

The original architectural plan—front view. Created in City Engineer W.E. Cutshaw's office. *Library of Virginia*.

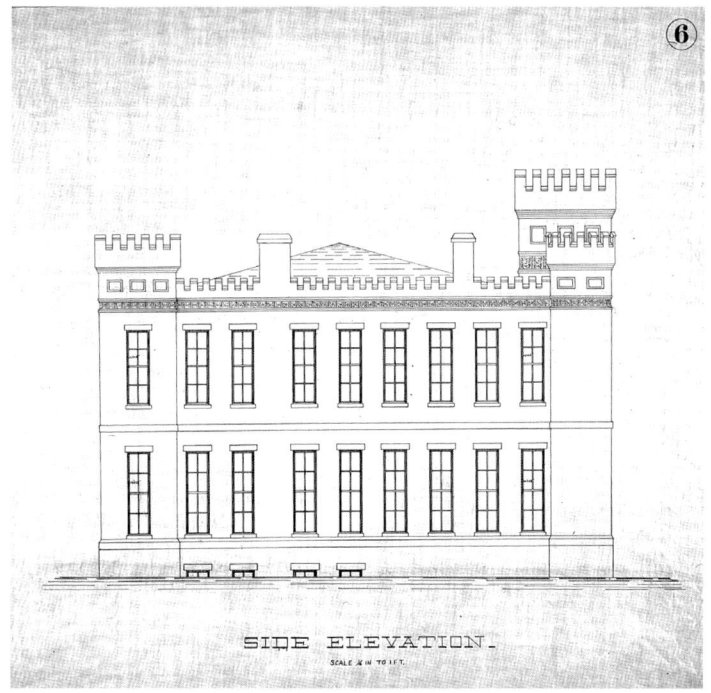

The original architectural plan—side view. Created in City Engineer W.E. Cutshaw's office. *Library of Virginia.*

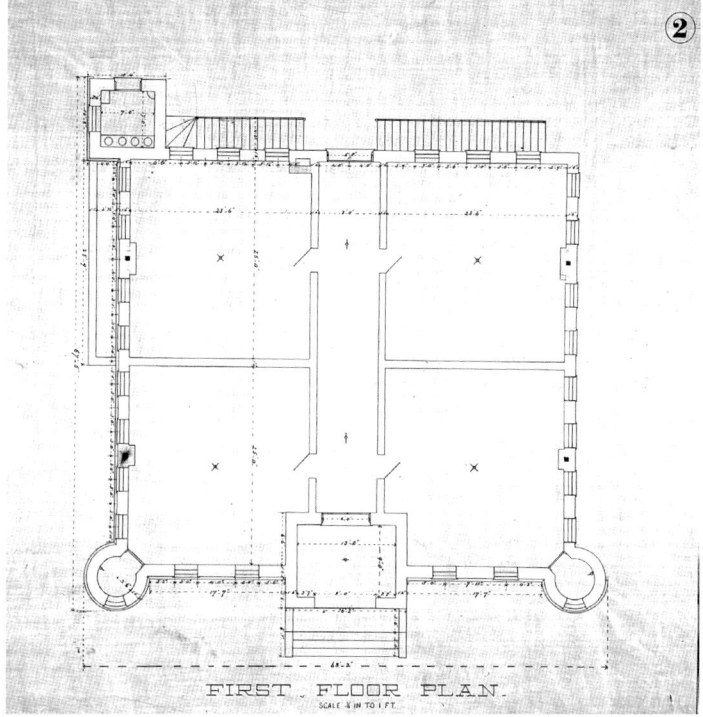

The original architectural plan—first floor. Created in City Engineer W.E. Cutshaw's office. *Library of Virginia.*

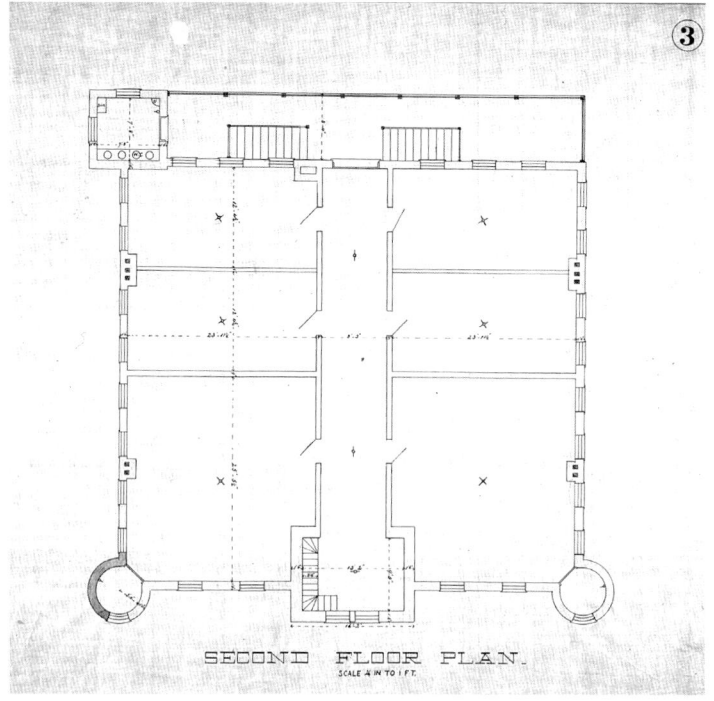

The original architectural plan—second floor. Created in City Engineer W.E. Cutshaw's office. *Library of Virginia.*

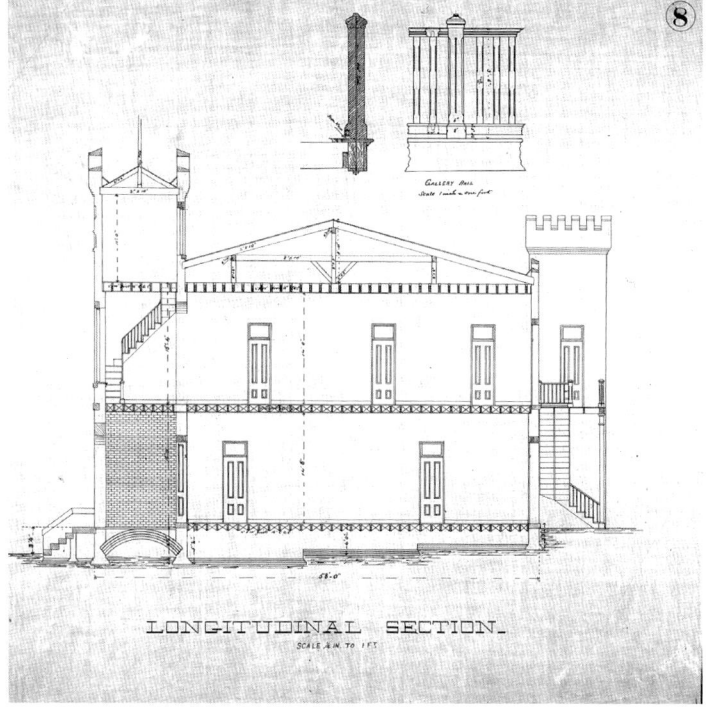

The original architectural plan—longitudinal cross-section view. Created in City Engineer W.E. Cutshaw's office. *Library of Virginia.*

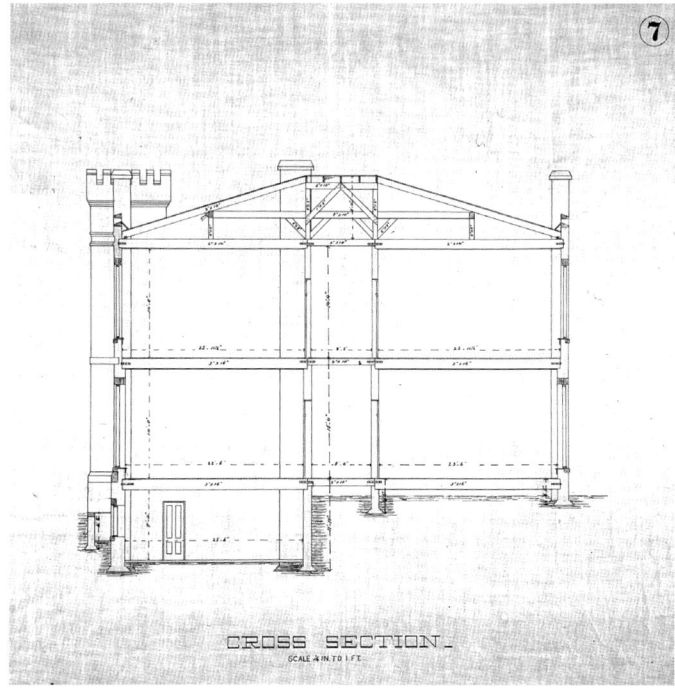

The original architectural plan—left to right cross-section view. Created in City Engineer W.E. Cutshaw's office. *Library of Virginia.*

council not only voted to fund the Armory but also overrode the mayor's veto of supplementary funding.

Richmond officials had planned to locate a shed in the space behind the Leigh Street Armory but never approved the monies to construct it. Despite the disappointment in this, the hope for a shed continued. Mitchell reflected this in his December 1895 summary article, noting that a ten-day bazaar had generated $175 to help fund the drill shed.[77] Ultimately, having no shed, Richmond's black militia companies resorted for the next several years to drilling in various locations around Richmond, outside in the space behind the Armory and on city streets.

## The Howitzer Armory—A Comparison

Adding the $4,000 for the land to the $10,000 for construction, the total cost for the Leigh Street Armory came to $14,000. The following description of the Howitzer Armory provides a fairly stark contrast to the Leigh Street Armory's more limited interior and scale:

> *The Armory is three stories high, with a sub-basement, containing engine-rooms, etc. It has a large gun-room, which is to have a granolithic flooring, a drill hall, and gallery, officers' rooms, library, large company-room, with lockers; tower-room, etc., and is said to be the handsomest armory for an individual company in the United States. Its appointments are perfect….The City Council appropriated $25,000…for the construction of the Armory, and it will require about $800 more to add a few improvements necessary to put the house in First-class condition for occupancy by the battery.[78]*

Not only did the council approve for the Howitzer Armory more than double the amount designated for the Leigh Street Armory, but its addition of supplementary funds suggests the concretization of whiteness as property, a theory articulated in the Supreme Court case of *Plessy v. Ferguson* (1896). The *Plessy* decision not only sanctioned separate but equal as constitutional and within the police power of the state but also established whiteness as property—the legal theory that whites were entitled to certain things, including superior physical accommodations, that blacks were not, simply because they were black. Or, rather, because they were not white. Thus, consistent with *Plessy* (which came a year following the Armory's construction), material improvements, special rooms, a drill shed and many other features of the Howitzer were not included in plans for the Leigh Street Armory.[79]

Richmond also built a spacious gymnasium-like drill shed for the 1910 Blues Armory, which it placed on the building's third floor. In the replacement building for the old First Regiment or Greys Armory, the city built a shed on the upper floor, as indicated in the following *Richmond Times-Dispatch* description: "The upper floor is given up mainly to the drill hall, 98 by 176 feet, which is believed to be ample for the maneuvers of the battalion. There is a cloak room and one for women visitors. A balcony floor to this hall has an association room for the meetings of the First Regiment Association, and a band room and band stand."[80]

## Debate over the Masonry Contract

After the bidding for doing the brickwork on the Leigh Street Armory was completed, the city awarded the contract to a team of black bricklayers headed up by Armistead Walker Jr. Walker was an African American, a master bricklayer and husband of black clubwoman and future president of the St. Luke Penny Savings Bank, Maggie Lena Walker. The awarding of the contract to a black contractor did not sit well with the white bricklayers' union, so it took its case to city council. The objections were mostly about racial preference, since the city had taken special care to ensure that it had taken all of the required steps for securing bids and letting contracts. The union argued, more than a little ironically, that it was wrong for black masons to win the contract to do the work on an armory to be built for black soldiers.[81]

Armistead Walker Jr. *Maggie L. Walker National Historic Site.*

Alderman Mitchell was in attendance and reported on this debate among the councilmen. He wrote that a white alderman complained, "These colored people think that they must be treated better.…I have no objection to anybody making a living. I stand as the representative of the white race. I promised those who sent me here to stand by the white race. I am in favor of white men doing the work."[82] As might be expected, Mitchell quoted in detail his own comments before the committee. At the beginning of his remarks, he displayed disdain for what the white bricklayers were asking the council to do. He wrote:

> *I have listened with much surprise at the remarks of the gentleman representing the white Bricklayers' Union and I am thoroughly convinced that he and his poor misguided brethren are laboring under a misapprehension. He comes here and asks that colored men be not allowed to work and that white ones be employed upon a job given out by contract. Such proposition is absurd. We know no colored, here, Mr. Chairman. During the six years that I have been connected with the city council, I have been proud to say that I have been treated in a manner that I was not even reminded that I was colored.*[83]

Mitchell then reminded the councilmen that he and the other black councilmen had supported their white colleagues throughout their time on the city council. And he noted painfully the inequities inherent in the city's funding priorities: "Out of more than $270,000 paid out to the employees in this city not three percent go into the pockets of colored people and now they want to bar us from work on the outside. We have wives and children to support, gentlemen."[84] Mitchell also observed that since the time of slavery, black citizens had worked hard to make a living. Finally, in an impassioned but rather sardonic closing comment, he spoke of the goodwill that had existed between black and white citizens over the decades, even invoking the memories of loyal, laboring black men and women during the Civil War. A week later, on March 16, Mitchell concluded his comments on the meeting, reporting that the debate was thus over. Armistead Walker and his team would complete the brickwork on the Leigh Street Armory.[85]

## Key Figures Secure Funding for the Armory

Based on Mitchell's summaries of the events leading up to construction of the Armory, three individuals—Mitchell himself, Major Joseph B. Johnson and Colonel W.E. Cutshaw—appear to have been especially pivotal in getting the City of Richmond to build the Armory. Brief profiles of each follow.

### *Editor John Mitchell Jr.*

John Mitchell Jr. was born into slavery in Richmond, Virginia, on July 11, 1863. He attended public school in Richmond and in 1881 graduated with high honors from the Richmond Normal and High School. He taught school in his early adult years, but in 1884, at the age of twenty-one, his career took a major turn. The *Richmond Planet* appointed him as its editor and publisher, in which capacity he served for forty-five years. Ironically, Mitchell's transition to editor of the *Planet* was providential, as it took place in the same year Richmond first approved funding to acquire land for the Armory.

Over the course of his years as editor of the *Planet*, Mitchell came to be known locally and nationally as the brave "fighting editor" who battled against lynching and injustice as Richmond and the South slid steadily into the era of Jim Crow and the Black Nadir. In addition to his work as editor, Mitchell served on Richmond City Council from 1888 to 1896. Election

John Mitchell Jr., circa early 1900s. *Library of Virginia.*

fraud, something that impacted many other black politicians across the South in that period, led to his defeat.[86]

In 1902, John Mitchell Jr. established Mechanics Savings Bank and served as its president until it went into receivership in 1922. In 1910, he built an impressive four-story bank building in the center of Richmond, a building that still stands today. From 1904 to 1921, he attended the meetings of the powerful and prestigious American Bankers Association (ABA)—the only black man to do so in those years. Mitchell attended those meetings regularly for seventeen years, traveling across the country to attend, first by train and, once he acquired his first Stanley Steamer automobile (he purchased three within five years) in 1918, often by car.[87] Notably, Mitchell wrote highly unique and detailed travelogues of his travels to these and other meetings, which he published in his newspaper.

Mitchell also owned a number of businesses, including a cemetery, a printing business and a theater. A local community leader, he was a major figure in the Knights of Pythias, a fraternal organization that was prominent both locally and nationally. Mitchell often led important public ceremonies and generally was seen as one of Richmond's leading black figures. He was also respected nationally within the black community as an outstanding example of business, culture and civil rights advocacy and leadership.[88]

In 1922, twenty years after Mitchell established the Mechanics Savings Bank, the State Corporation Commission put his bank into receivership. This led to a painful few years during which he suffered serious legal threats, the loss of much of his wealth and a decline in reputation. He died diminished, but undefeated, on December 3, 1929, while still the editor of his newspaper and president of his bank.[89]

## *Major Joseph B. Johnson*

Major Johnson, who descended from free blacks in Virginia, worked as a mechanic at the time his military career began. In 1882, which was relatively early in his time as a militia member, the Volunteers promoted him to the rank of major. Johnson then emerged as the highest-ranking African American militia officer in Virginia. The Virginia Volunteers had promoted other black officers to the rank of major. However, by the time the city built the Armory, he was the most senior black officer within the Volunteers. In the years preceding the Armory's construction, Major Johnson was undoubtedly the most important figure—in addition to Mitchell—among those who helped persuade the city first to buy the land in 1884 and, with Mitchell's help, to build the Armory in 1895.

After the completion of the Armory, Johnson's leadership role in Richmond's militia continued for just over three years more. In 1898, he volunteered to serve in the Spanish-American War and again was appointed to the rank of major, this time to command the First Battalion within the U.S. Army's all-black Sixth Virginia Regiment. Johnson served successfully and faithfully in this capacity for the nearly seven months the black troops trained for war, after which time Virginia disbanded its black militias. He is without doubt the most prominent African American military figure to emerge from this phase of Virginia's history and, as such, was a true trailblazer and a successful, respected leader in a period of enormous change and racial turmoil in Virginia.

Mitchell quite obviously considered Johnson to be a very significant leader within the community. In his December 21, 1895 summary on how the Armory came to be, Mitchell provided a fairly detailed and complementary profile on Johnson. He first referred to his early years, writing:

> *Major Joseph Brown Johnson was born in Amelia County, Virginia, on March 12, 1847. His parents, Amanda and Anderson Johnson, being free moved to Manchester in 1859, bringing young Johnson with eight other children, consisting of five girls and four boys. While quite young he was put to work under Mr. Thomas Mann, now residing in Manchester, after which he was employed in Mr. James Fisher's tobacco factory until the beginning of the war. He received his Exemption papers from the Confederate Government, exempting him from draft on Government works. He then sought employment with view of getting his trade at the Bell Island Iron Works.*
>
> *During this time he became thirsty for knowledge, and attended private night school taught by Mr. David Bowers, who was a student himself. The circumstances of the times, and the laws of the state prohibiting the instruction of colored persons, he abandoned any further teaching of young Johnson.*
>
> *The late Ballard T. Edwards had a night school at his home in Manchester, unknown to the authorities and the young man attended this school under many disadvantages until 1862.*[90]

Mitchell then turned to the major's rapid rise through the ranks in his military career. Johnson enlisted in 1871, the first year Virginia opened membership to black volunteers. He entered the "Volunteer Service of Virginia," Mitchell explained, "as a private in the Union Guards, Co. C." The state recognized each militia company, both by its self-designated name (in this case, the Union Guards) and by a letter (Company C). The latter reflected the order in which a given company formed. The state did the letter sequencing separately for white versus black companies, battalions and so on. Thus, being the third formed within the battalion, the Union Guard was Company C, Colored.[91]

A year later, in June 1872, Johnson's company elected him junior second lieutenant, for which he received his commission a year later, in June 1873. From there, he continued to rise within the ranks. In February 1874, Johnson's company elected him first lieutenant, a position that he held for eight years until 1882, when he was elected captain. Johnson served only a short while as captain, as he was destined to rise yet again to the highest position of leadership within the battalion. Two years after his appointment as first lieutenant, Virginia, in June 1876, organized the First Battalion and appointed a man with the same last name, R.H. Johnson, as major. In 1882, Major R.H. Johnson resigned his position (shortly after J.B. Johnson had become captain), and the process of electing a new battalion leader began.[92]

J.B. Johnson did not seek that particular leadership position, Mitchell explained. Rather, he said, the position was "urged upon him." Here is how Mitchell explained what happened: "Major R.H. Johnson having resigned, the contest for Major was then opened. Captain Johnson being the Junior Captain had no idea of entering the contest or neither did he want it, but his abilities being noticed by his friends who urged upon him to allow his name to be used, he was elected Major June 26, 1882 unanimously."[93]

It was not easy serving in leadership positions within the black units in those years. As Mitchell noted, the battalion was very much underfunded and thus lacked the needed equipment, uniforms and, overall, the level of training and support the state typically provided to its white units. Mitchell explained that the battalion "at that time was in a very poor condition, as to drills, uniform, discipline and proper organization. The officers lacked harmony." Despite this, he said, the "new Major bent his energy toward discipline, beginning with the officers, six of whom had to be put under arrest within thirty days after his election and three court-martialed and dismissed from the service."[94]

Of course, Mitchell wrote the above about Johnson in 1895. He thus could not yet have covered the important three years after the battalion occupied the Armory or the consequential time Johnson served in the Spanish-American War. This was a dramatic and short-lived period of service, a time when Major Johnson emerged as a steady leader in the face of significant racial turmoil.

## Colonel Wilfred E. Cutshaw

Colonel W.E. Cutshaw served as Richmond's city engineer from 1874 to 1907. In this time, he had a major impact on the development of Richmond. The National Park Service summarized his many contributions as follows:

> *Wilfred Emory Cutshaw, who oversaw the building's design and construction, was a grand figure in the development of Richmond. During his 34-year tenure as City Engineer, Cutshaw's endeavors included roads, sidewalks, schools, armories, parks, markets, and the construction of Old City Hall, one of the city's most magnificent buildings. He was an advocate for tree planting along streets, and oversaw the creation of a tree nursery at the Byrd Park Reservoir. In 1907, a reporter for the* Richmond Times-Dispatch *wrote that "Cutshaw's greatest ambition was to turn every available foot of space into recreation resorts for the public."* [95]

Of course, Cutshaw played a pivotal role in facilitating construction of the Leigh Street Armory, not only by providing technical support as an architect and planner but also, possibly more importantly, by providing respected advice and counsel to the city's leadership at key moments when decisions about whether to go forward with construction were being made. John Mitchell Jr. recognized that without Cutshaw's backing, Richmond City Council might never have approved the Armory's construction. Cutshaw was a key player in securing funding for purchasing land for the Armory, finding the site on which to build it, providing the design for it, promoting approval for the supplementary $2,500 to help with construction and generally overseeing the project.

In his 2002 application for the Armory to be placed in the National Register of Historic Places, Selden Richardson provided further detail on Cutshaw's essential role in both promoting and designing the building:

> *The First Battalion Virginia Volunteers armory was designed in the office of Richmond City Engineer Cutshaw, and was part of an extensive building program under Cutshaw during the 1890s that saw the construction of several Richmond armories, schools and markets. The drawings from Cutshaw's office for both the as-built structure and a one-story alternative design survive in the collection of the Library of Virginia, and from these it can be seen that the building that stands on Leigh Street is faithful to the original design. The appearance of*

City engineer colonel W.E. Cutshaw. *Library of Virginia.*

*the First Battalion Virginia Volunteers closely follows the decorative scheme of two other armories built by Cutshaw during this period. Both the Richmond Howitzers' Battalion Armory (1895, demolished circa 1971) and the First Regiment Cavalry Virginia Volunteers Armory (1895, demolished circa 1970) shared identical crenellated towers with distinctive panels.*[96]

In his December 1895 historical summary of the Armory, Mitchell wrote the following about Cutshaw and his importance relative to the building:

> *The structure is a handsome one and the troops are proud of it. Thanks are extended to that liberal white element that buried their prejudices and recognized the justness of the plea for substantial recognition.*
>
> *In this matter Col. W.E. Cutshaw has been a tireless friend, and it is to him and assistant City Engineer Bates that credit is due for such a handsome structure as ornaments St. Peter and Leigh Sts.*[97]

The next year, Mitchell again praised Cutshaw on the front page of the *Planet*, this time even more lavishly, writing:

> *Col. W.E. Cutshaw, our present City Engineer is one of the most remarkable characters in the city government to-day. His powers as an organizer and his abilities as a city official are conceded. Candid to the point of bluntness, conscientious to the point of stubbornness, a friend to his friends and an enemy relentless to those who would wrongfully tamper with the people's interests, he stands forth as the power behind the throne, and a tower of strength in any contest.*
>
> *His democracy is unquestioned and yet he is just. Color forms no bar to courteous treatment at his hands.*
>
> *He was a warm supporter of the proposition to erect the colored armory and when the amount appropriated was insufficient to ensure the erection of a handsome and substantial structure, it was he who put on foot the plans for an authorization of $2500 more, recommended it and successfully used his powerful influence to secure its passage. The Mayor's veto notwithstanding.*[98]

The irony cannot be overstated that Cutshaw, a white man who served as a Confederate officer in the Civil War, played such a pivotal role in ensuring that the historic black armory would be built in Richmond.

## The Armory and the Community

With the Armory construction complete in October 1895, Richmond officials handed over the building's keys to the First Battalion in a grand ceremony in the Armory. The occasion appears to have been both solemn and officious, befitting the turnover of an important military structure to its intended occupants. Summarizing the event in the *Planet*, Mitchell wrote that the hardworking Committee on Grounds and Buildings met on Saturday, October 5, "at the new armory, First Battalion, Va. Volunteers to formally turn over this handsome structure to Major J.B. Johnson and his corps of officers."[99] The committee then joined others, including battalion leaders and Mitchell, on an inspection tour of the building. Afterward, they all gathered for the ceremony on the "large porch on the second floor where the Committee on Grounds and Buildings met."[100]

First, Colonel Cutshaw made some remarks, commenting on the "difficulties under which they had labored." He also "spoke of the liability of the contract of which the committee subsequently relieved him."[101] This latter point suggests that Cutshaw oversaw implementation of the construction contract, which, of course, had at that point been fulfilled. Cutshaw's comment also suggests that the long task of seeing the Armory to completion was onerous.

The *Planet* then reported Cutshaw's observation that "the colored troops had demonstrated their efficiency upon more than one occasion. He spoke of the quick response when called to the penitentiary and their soldierly bearing at Newport News." The first instance referred, as discussed earlier, to the performance of Richmond's State Guard, a Richmond black militia unit that the governor had sent, along with other troops, to help quell a riot at a Newport News shipyard. The second referred to Richmond's black Carney Guard that was among the first militia units to arrive at Richmond's Libby Prison following an earthquake that damaged the prison walls. In referencing these, Cutshaw clearly recognized how important it was in securing funding for the Armory that the African American soldiers avoided controversies and performed as loyal citizens within the community.[102]

Major Johnson then responded to Cutshaw's remarks about the troop's performance. He said "that the troops under his command would always prove faithful to the trust and respond whenever called upon." He then "thanked the officials, the committee and the city council for the handsome building which had been entrusted to his keeping as commanding officer." At that point, Mitchell recorded, the city officials turned the keys over to the battalion leadership, and the ceremony ended.[103]

The plan was for the battalion officially to take control of the building on the sixteenth of that month. Two dates thus mark the official opening of the Armory: the day when the council handed over the keys to the battalion leaders, on October 5, and the day the battalion occupied the building, eleven days later, on October 16.

In his October 19 edition of the *Richmond Planet*, Mitchell provided a memorable description of the Armory's appearance at night, a description that has since become a kind of benediction, solemnizing the culmination of over ten years of struggle to secure funding for this extraordinary building: "On last Wednesday night, the beautifully lighted armory could be seen from this section glowing in magnificent splendor. A few minutes past 8 o'clock the tap of the drum told us that the Battalion was about to enter."[104]

The *Dispatch* also published a glowing review of the new armory. It described it in warm and complimentary terms, saying it was "large, roomy, and substantially built." It also observed that "that part of the city is much beautified by this fine building.…With its large centre-tower, circular cornertowers, and granite and terra-cotta trimmings, it is a work for the city to be proud of." The *Dispatch* even acknowledged that "there has long been need for this armory for the colored troop" and pointed to the commitment of those of "the colored race" who "enlisted in the volunteer service." Such commitment, the paper suggested, would "doubtless be much strengthened now that they will have a neat and handsome place to store their arms and uniforms, and they will take greater pride in keeping their accoutrements in first-class order."[105]

The *Richmond Planet* advertised repeatedly the events that would celebrate the handover of the Armory. The following was a typical entry:

> NEW ARMORY
> ST. PETER & LEIGH STS MILITARY BAZAAR
> Grand Opening of the New Armory, First Batt. Va. Vols. Inf Beginning Mon. Oct, 21. Continuing to Friday November First. New and Bright Attractions each Night Competitive Drills Richmond Female Cadets vs. Manchester Female Rifles.[106]

The "New Armory" announces a "Military Bazaar" to celebrate the official opening of the Armory. Published in the *Richmond Planet*, October 12, 1895, p. 1. *Library of Virginia.*

From October 21 through November 1, organizers scheduled something special for each weekday evening. The first night's grand opening, for instance, featured a concert by the Battalion band and an opportunity for the public to inspect the building. The band also played each night over the course of the two weeks.

Bands were often featured in concerts and parades in that era. At that time, both militia and fraternal order bands were active and often marched in the same parades. Long after the black militias disbanded in 1899, the fraternal bands continued to perform in Richmond.

The event also featured "goods and wares" for sale "at city prices," refreshments, a raffle of male and female bicycles, a reward for the person selling the most tickets, musical programs (e.g., Manchester and Richmond mandolin clubs competed), a reception for ministers and "literary entertainment." The admission charge was ten cents. Of course, the celebrations also included military displays, maneuvering, contests and inspections in which each of the three Richmond-based militia companies participated. Fraternal organizations—the Knights of Pythias and Knights of Damon—also performed, as did several female cadet corps. (The story of the female cadet corps begs for scholarly attention.)

As with Mitchell's descriptions of the parades, because he held very high leadership positions in the Knights of Pythias, he frequently reported on the body's many activities in his newspaper. It is primarily from such reporting that we learn of the fraternal organizations' participation in parades and community celebrations, such as Emancipation Day and the Fourth of July, well into the early twentieth century.

In July of the next year, the community held a similar two-week event at the Armory's "spacious drill grounds." It does not appear, however, that it put on similar events in 1897, 1898 or, certainly, 1899, the year Richmond converted the building into an elementary school.

In his December 21, 1895 summary on the Armory, Mitchell wrote that a ladies' club donated a clock to the Armory:

> *On Wednesday, December 4th, as the officers of the Battalion were conducting their regular monthly meeting, the undersigned ladies of the Twilight club, filed into the officers' headquarters with a handsome clock for the armory, which was presented and replied to in a neat speech by Lieut. H.L. Harris, M.D. A hearty vote of thanks was tendered by the board of officers. The ladies left with a feeling of happiness that they had accomplished something more for the Soldier Boys.*[107]

Relatively few women are mentioned as having a role, symbolic or otherwise, in the Armory's planning, construction or operations. Mitchell took care to record the names of the women involved in his paper, hopefully out of esteem for the clubwomen's activity of the day. He listed the leadership of the women's organization as Miss Catherine Mosby, president; Miss Eveline Edwards, vice president; Mrs. Ella Claiborne, treasurer; Mrs. W.T. Edwards, secretary; Misses Susie E. Taylor and Mattie

Anderson; and Mesdames Sarah Johnson, Mary Hostley, Sarah Fleming and Martha Cunningham.[108]

Since no Armory artifacts are known to remain, aside from the building itself, one can only wonder about the nature and history of the gifted clock and, more importantly, of the interactions between local women and the militia over the content and interior of the Armory. Given this brief, gendered look into the Armory's value to the community that surrounded it, it would be valuable to know what other roles women—and the African American community at large—played in the Armory's life before its conversion to a school. It would also be of interest to know what other decorations and furnishings the battalion placed in the building.

It should come as no surprise that the Leigh Street Armory, with its distinctive visage and function, would become an important source of community pride. Not only did it provide a dignified place in which the First Battalion's soldiers could meet and train, but it also served as a central place for major gatherings and special events. It also provided a powerful reminder of the civil rights Richmond's black citizens believed they had gained, a view, of course, that tightening racial segregation was rapidly eroding. Unfortunately, while the community rightly felt pride in the Armory, it could not have foreseen that its central place in community gatherings and celebrations would be dramatically transformed just over three years later.

CHAPTER 4

# FAITHFUL TO THE TRUST

## The Spanish-American War

In January 1898, little more than two years after completion of the Armory, the United States military sent a fairly new cruiser ship, the USS *Maine*, to Cuba's Havana Harbor. The United States thus signaled its intent to protect its interests against a Spanish takeover of that small island nation. But on the evening of February 15, 1898, the unexpected happened. A violent explosion shook the ship, sinking it rapidly and killing nearly three-fourths of its crew. The event drew the United States directly into war with Spain. America's "yellow press" immediately began to fan the flames of war, blaming the explosion on Spain, even though the cause was unknown. "Remember the *Maine*, to Hell with Spain" became the rally cry that led the nation into the Spanish-American War.[109] While the navy was relatively well prepared for this war, the army was not. To strengthen the regular army forces, President William McKinley ordered a call-up of men, including a large number of volunteer militia members.

Initially, Virginia was expected to provide three regiments of volunteers. In response, members of the black militia units began immediately to volunteer. In April 1898, however, Virginia governor James Hoge Tyler, facing resistance from his white constituency, choose to enlist white soldiers only. As will be seen, this was only the first of a number of racial struggles in which Virginia's black citizens and troops would become embroiled in this politically and symbolically important opportunity for them to serve their country.

# Richmond's Leigh Street Armory & African American Militia

*Above*: The USS *Maine*, second class battleship, in Havana Harbor, Cuba, shortly before the 1898 explosion that precipitated America's war with Spain. *Wikipedia.*

*Right*: African American soldiers in Cuba, circa 1899. *Library of Congress.*

## Editor Mitchell's "No Officers, No Fight!"

Throughout those first months when the governor of Virginia struggled over the call-up of black troops, John Mitchell Jr. editorialized aggressively about the issue. He first focused on the inappropriateness of blacks volunteering to fight at all, given the growing assault on their rights at home. Then, as recruitment and preparations for war continued and the black soldiers expressed eagerness to enlist, his focus shifted to the question of black officers commanding black troops. Both arguments appeared, for example, in an editorial Mitchell published in early May 1898, when recruitment was again getting underway. Here he fervently expressed his deep cynicism about the antipathy of white leaders toward the black troops:

> *A race of people who, denied the right of suffrage, outraged, butchered with their rights ruthlessly trampled upon from one end of the south to the other, that would kiss the hand that smites, and beg the privilege of dying for their oppressors is degenerate indeed, and can but merit the contempt of the people in whose cause they enlist.*
>
> *Again, we voice the cry, one that we have repeatedly uttered during the past ten years: A man who is not good enough to vote for a government is not good enough to fight for it.*[110]

Here Mitchell identified the ultimate contradiction—asking African American men to defend their country, while at the same time the nation abrogated its Fifteenth Amendment protections against race, color and slave-based denial or circumvention of voting rights. Richmond, by this time, actively disenfranchised black voters. This was something Mitchell, having lost his position on Richmond City Council to white efforts to suppress the black vote, understood perfectly.

Mitchell was also good at introducing sarcasm when the opportunity and need to do so presented itself. He wrote:

> *For our part, we are perfectly willing to let the white folks do the dying, and we do the living.*
>
> *White men, rally 'round the flag! Die for your country! We'll take care of your families as we did thirty years ago, and hang any man who maltreats or outrages them. Leave your business, and work-shops! On to the front! Colored men, no officers; no fight!*[111]

Mitchell's "no officers, no fight" mantra quickly became a galvanizing catchphrase both locally and nationally for the struggle over black participation in the Spanish-American War.

A month later, in early June 1898, Mitchell used both better management and constitutional arguments to press for the appointment of black officers. Notably, he used the Fourteenth Amendment's equal justice clause to make his point. He reasoned that if white troops could have white officers, black troops and officers should have that right as well:

> *Immediately there is a demand from the Negro-hating element that the colored officers be made to step aside and white men who do not know the companies, or had any part in their instruction shall be appointed majors, captains, lieutenants, etc.*
>
> *This is done too in the face of the fact that the second, third, and forth regiments of Virginia Volunteers have white officers. There is not a colored officer in any of these white companies.*
>
> *Now it is proposed to draw the color line, violate the Fourteenth Amendment to the Constitution of the United States by removing the officers, because they are colored, and appoint others in their stead because they are white.*
>
> *No wonder that the Chief Executive of the state who, but a few days ago, swore to recognize the civil and political equality of all men before the law stands aghast at such a proposition, and refuses to violate the guarantees of the Constitution of the United States and the Bill of Rights of Virginia.*[112]

In mid-June of that year, after President McKinley issued a second call for troops and urged governors to enlist black volunteers, Governor Tyler relented and agreed not only to enlist soldiers from Virginia's two black battalions but also to bring forward their militia officers who would serve at battalion and company levels. Those two battalions were then to be formed into an all-black regiment: the Sixth Virginia Volunteers Infantry. The governor also chose a commissioned white officer, Colonel Richard C. Croxton, to command at the regiment level the black soldiers of the Sixth Virginia. Croxton proved to be an insensitive and tactless leader. As a result, his appointment added measurably to tensions over the appointment of black officers for the Sixth Virginia's truncated life—a period of approximately seven months.[113]

Editor Mitchell then reported that the governor had reversed his position and agreed to appoint black officers. "Gov. J. Hoge Tyler has decided that the Colored troops shall be commanded by their own Colored Officers. To remove them he declares would be to violate his oath of office, and he cannot comply with the wishes of those who made the demand upon him."[114]

Mitchell also offered a possible explanation for why there had been such staunch opposition to the appointment of black officers—that they would be earning the higher salaries that would otherwise be available to white officers:

> *Major J.B. Johnson of Richmond will command the First Battalion, Virginia Volunteer Infantry, and Major W.H. Johnson of Petersburg will command the Second Battalion, Virginia Volunteer Infantry. The War Department has decided to muster in both officers and men as they are. The Salary of a Major in the regular army is said to be about Three Thousand Dollars per year. This no doubt accounts for the opposition. Gov. Tyler, of Virginia, Sir!*[115]

Despite past and ongoing discrimination and segregation, the opportunity to serve instilled within the black volunteers an expectation of change, a hope the community demonstrated with overt and proud

displays of patriotism. Reporting on the recruitment process in July 1898, for instance, the *Planet* wrote, with obvious enthusiasm, that the "fine new armory of the First Battalion, Virginia Volunteers Infantry has been the scene of much activity during this week." It explained that the War Department had agreed to muster in black troops and to allow black officers. The latter meant, however, officers at the battalion, not the regiment level. To allow black officers at a higher level, military historian John Listman explained, would have required them to appoint black soldiers to ranks higher than major. Had they not agreed to appointing black officers at the battalion level, Mitchell argued, the black soldiers would not have volunteered.[116]

By the end of June 1898, Mitchell was still upbeat about the prospects for the black volunteers. With obvious enthusiasm, he wrote, "Things around the Armory had been assuming a warlike appearance all the week. Some faces are wreathed in smiles because they were successful in passing the physical

The Sixth Virginia on its mobilization day, June 20, 1898. *Virginia State University.* "Likely taken at Camp Corbin, the mobilization site for all four Virginia regiments taken into federal service during the Spanish-American War. Note the medal on the officer's chest in the foreground was a company or unit, not a Virginia State award." *Caption by John W. Listman Jr.*

examination while others were not so happy."[117] His remark hinted at the difficulties some black volunteers were encountering during the exams. Still, he presumed many would qualify to serve:

> *Our boys had to be more carefully examined than our white friends. We have been informed that the authorities were censured for sending some of that trash from Virginia and as usual the colored boys must make up for it.*
>
> *Well we are going and be healthy and proportionately built too. The stalwart fine, looking soldiers of color sent from Richmond will be a credit to Virginia and doubtless the white officers will wish they were in command.*[118]

It became readily apparent, however, that many of the black troops and the other volunteers could not pass their physicals, were too old to enlist or simply preferred not to enlist. As a result, as Ann Field Alexander pointed out in her article on the Virginia militia, only one in six of the approximately eight hundred black soldiers recruited in July and August 1898 to serve two-year stints came from the existing militia units.[119]

Also, because many of the black recruits accepted for training were inexperienced and untrained, they were, for the most part, unprepared for the rigors they would face in a regimented military environment. They would have seasoned officers from the leadership ranks of the two black battalions and their companies, but the troops themselves were mostly ill prepared for what they were about to experience at camp.

A week later, Mitchell published the following letter that he had sent to the secretary of war regarding the appointment of black officers:

> *Dear Sir:—I see it stated that it is not the policy of the government to place colored officers in command of colored troops, and that companies of state troops with colored officers are to be mustered in only with white officers.*
>
> *Please advise whether or not this is the policy of your department.*[120]

Many of the "Colored Troops" failed their physicals. *Richmond Planet,* July 2, 1898, p. 1. *Library of Virginia.*

Mitchell immediately published the following response received from the assistant adjunct general:

> Sir:—In reply to your letter of 7*th* instant, I have the honor to inform you that the Government has laid down no definite policy in regard to the commissioned officers of colored troops.

# Richmond's Leigh Street Armory & African American Militia

An unknown first sergeant, circa 1898. *Virginia State University.* "He is wearing an unknown (non–state issued) medal. His uniform consists of five-button field blouse and tan felt campaign hat." *Caption by John W. Listman Jr.*

> *There are companies and battalions of state troops in service with colored officers, and also with white officers and there are regiments of U.S. Volunteers in which the field, staff and captains are white and the lieutenants colored.*[121]

Despite the apparent resolution of the conflict surrounding the appointment of black officers in June of that year, the struggle over officers reignited again a few months later—specifically, while at camp in Tennessee. The struggle continued until the government mustered the black Virginia-based soldiers out of service in January 1899 and disbanded the militia units a few months thereafter.

## Three Camps in Six Months—Beginning at Camp Corbin

The military moved Virginia's black soldiers between three camps within the mere six months they served in the Spanish-American War. The sites were Camp Corbin near Richmond; Camp Poland near Knoxville, Tennessee;

and Camp Haskell near Macon, Georgia. Things started off relatively peacefully for the troops, although racial tensions spiked once they arrived in Knoxville and persisted after they moved to Macon.

By late July 1898, the Sixth Virginia had set up at Camp Corbin, conveniently located about ten miles southeast of Richmond. Being close to home, the camp provided a comfortable setting within which the mostly raw troops could adjust to the challenges inherent in preparing for war. They could make authorized trips back and forth from the city, which helped to maintain both troop morale and connections to family and community.

Almost weekly, the *Planet* published reports on life in camp, a pattern of reporting that continued for the duration of the troops' encampment. These reports commented mostly on the routine and rigors of living and training in camp, as well as the soldiers' hope and expectation that they would be sent to the front lines. When they transferred from Camp Corbin to Knoxville several months later, the soldiers' reports focused far more on the unpleasant details surrounding the racial conflicts the regiment encountered.

One First Battalion officer, in particular, wanted those beyond the camp to know what was going on. How better to do this than to write serially to the editor of the *Planet*? Using the pseudonym "Ham," this officer sent many of the reports that Mitchell published prominently in the weekly newspaper.

Detail of officers of the Sixth Virginia on mobilization day, June 20, 1898. *Virginia State University.* "Probably taken at Camp Corbin, the mobilization site for each of the four Virginia regiments during the Spanish-American War. These likely are members of the 2nd Battalion, since Major William H. Johnson owned this image." *Caption by John W. Listman Jr.*

Ham's first letter, dated July 26, 1898, began by attesting to the sacrifice of the recruits:

> *Companies E. and F. of Petersburg under command of Captains Hill and Webb respectively, have reached camp and where once was a wilderness is now a tented city filled with the life and enthusiasm from the boys in blue, who have given up their homes and are preparing to risk their lives in the defense of their country's honor....We now have 525 men in camp, and a happier or more contented lot would be hard to find. The battalion has thrown into the Sixth Regiment and quite a large number of appointments and promotions have been made on this account.*[122]

As might be expected, Ham's early reports primarily described camp conditions, commenting on such things as weather, soldiers' health, issues with food and other similar concerns unique to the experience. Overall, the reports were upbeat and hopeful about what lay ahead.

Ham's August 8 report noted that the numbers of recruits, representing both the First and Second Battalions, had risen from the 525 reported in July to about 850. His report provided still more insight into the everyday experiences of life in camp. He said that the men had received "wholesome" rations that they cooked on their own, with "little grumbling" being heard about this. Two springs supplied their needs for cooking and drinking, "one of light and the other of iron water." They bathed in two ponds, "which they [were] required to visit at least twice a week."[123]

Ham also spoke of the frustrations of living in the rugged, makeshift conditions of military camp. Pay and the weather were often highest on the list of complaints. "A visit from the paymaster about this time would be highly appreciated by the boys as nearly everyone is dead broke," he wrote. He said that because of a "severe rain storm a few days ago, two tents belonging to companies B and C were partially submerged with water and the occupants had to vacate them. The men have rendered this, however, by digging the trenches around their tents a little deeper." Living in tents in the woods, in the heat of a late Virginia summer, obviously produced much discomfort and tedium.[124]

Also in those early reports, Ham wrote of the inter-company rivalries, which mostly focused on which performed the best in drills, an assessment of which, he said, was "hard to determine, as all are eager to learn the manual and different movements." It was becoming increasingly apparent that the men were tiring of the stress and daily routines at camp. While

Two unidentified NCOs of the Sixth Virginia Volunteer Infantry at Camp Poland, Tennessee, in 1898. *Virginia State University.* "The man seated is a first sergeant and the one standing is a quartermaster sergeant. Since the image belonged to Major William H. Johnson of Petersburg who commanded the 2nd Battalion, composed mostly of men from that city, they are probably members of that battalion." *Caption by John W. Listman Jr.*

their spirits remained high at this stage of training, they were anxious to learn what the future held for them. They especially looked forward to being sent to the front lines, where they would "have an opportunity to distinguish themselves."[125]

On August 12, 1898, six months after the sinking of the *Maine*, Spain and the United States signed an armistice that brought hostilities to an end. Negotiations then continued between the two countries, concluding in the signing of a formal peace treaty in Paris on December 10 and ratification of that treaty by the U.S. Senate in early February 1899. Even with the early reporting of the treaty in August, the troops in training still faced the prospect of being sent to Cuba or the Philippines to serve in some military capacity. On the other hand, the talks continued and the war's end in the later months of 1898 was uncertain. So the role the soldiers would play was at that time unknown to them.

Ham reported that the army ordered the regiment to Camp Poland in Knoxville, a decision that the troops very much welcomed. New opportunities and, possibly, fewer drudgeries at camp signaled progress. The men expected that this new camp would be much better equipped and the conditions more accommodating. Ham wrote, "This will be a welcome change. The location of this Camp is very healthy, and abundance of water and good air; but a change of scenery and surroundings will have a tendency to make the men take more interest in their work."[126]

## Racial Conflict and Resignations at Camp Poland

Things started off well in Knoxville. In his first substantive report of life at Camp Poland, Ham wrote, "We are well satisfied with our lot, but the suspense is awful, no one can tell when or where we may be sent; however, all are willing and ready to go whenever our services may be required—whether in Cuba, [Puerto] Rico, or the Philippine[.]" As before, Ham focused on the everyday experiences of the troops. He even added the following small, but interesting, detail about life in camp: "No whiskey is allowed in camp, and positively no gambling." Whether Camp Corbin had allowed alcohol in camp was never addressed.[127]

Upon arrival at Knoxville's Camp Poland, the Sixth Virginia Volunteers were seemingly well received. The local white press reported that as the men passed in review, they were commended for their splendid appearance, military bearing and good physique. However, the men's transfer to this larger camp introduced a new set of circumstances, the implications of which members of the Sixth Virginia apparently did not anticipate. Based on Ham's next report from the new location, the regiment camped for the first time near white regiments, a situation that automatically heightened racial tensions. His report from Knoxville, however, did hint at the possibility of trouble, writing, only somewhat reassuringly, of the initial lack of any disturbance.[128]

That changed very soon, as within days a black regiment from North Carolina and a white one from Georgia engaged in a two-hour battle, firing their weapons in each other's direction, although apparently with little mortal intent. The skirmish, fortunately, injured no one. Two weeks after arriving in Knoxville, things took a dramatic turn for the Sixth Virginia, and chiefly for the officers of the Second Battalion. The *Planet* prefaced a startling telegraphic report sent from camp with an ominous observation, "The following telegraphic dispatch shows that the enemies of the Sixth Virginia Regiment have been at work at Washington":

> *Nine colored officers of the Sixth Virginia Volunteers to-day tendered their resignations to General McKee, commanding the Second Division, First Corps. They were Major W.H. Johnson, Captains Charles B. Nicolas, Jas. C. Hill, Jas. A.C. Stevens, Edward W. Gould, and Peter Shephard, Jr., and Lieutenants Samuel B. Randolph, Geo. T. Wright, and David Worrell. This wholesale resignation is attributed*

# Richmond's Leigh Street Armory & African American Militia

Captain John A.C. Stevens (*left*) and Major William H. Johnson at Camp Poland, Tennessee, 1898. *Virginia State University*. "Prior to the war, Stevens commanded the 'Petersburg Blues,' then designated as Company C, 2nd Battalion. When the Sixth Virginia was organized in July 1898, Company C, 2nd Battalion became Company G, 2nd Battalion, 6th VA. Both men resigned and returned to Petersburg on 15 October 1898." *Caption by John W. Listman Jr.*

Captain John A.C. Stevens of Petersburg's Company C, Second Battalion, in 1895. *Virginia State University.* "Captain Stevens took command of Petersburg's Company C when Major William H. Johnson in 1895 became major. Stevens was one of nine black officers to resign and return home in October 1898. In this studio portrait, he is wearing the Model 1895 officer's forge cap and officer's undress tunic. Note the 'VIRGINIA' embroidered under the eagle on his cap was a common feature of uniforms of the time." *Caption by John W. Listman Jr.*

> *to the fact that yesterday General McKee detailed a board of examiners to investigate and report concerning the qualifications, capacity, and efficiency of the above named officers.*[129]

All nine aforementioned officers in the Second Battalion resigned in protest of the pending investigation into their qualifications. The *Planet*'s front-page story of October 15, 1898, provided further details on the crisis:

> *Quite a sensation was caused in Camp last Wednesday by the resignation of nine of our officers. The order for the examination of the officers, as to their fitness, qualifications and conduct was issued Monday evening. By Tuesday afternoon every single officer affected by the order had tendered his resignation to Col. Croxton....The resignations have been forwarded to the President, and much speculation is indulged in as to what the result will be. According to rules and regulations, if the resignations are accepted, the appointments will be made from the ranks on the recommendation of the Regimental commander, the Governor of the State and the President.*[130]

Notably, Croxton did not recommend the First Battalion's officers be subjected to the same review, the reasons for which were not provided. Historian Ann Field Alexander points out in her article entitled "No

Edward V. Gould commanded Norfolk's National Guard company. *Virginia State University.* "The 'National Guard,' organized in January 1879, was originally designated Company E, 2nd Battalion. It was reorganized and redesignated Company D of the 6th Virginia in 1898 during the Spanish-American War. Gould served as its commander for this entire 19 year period." *Caption by John W. Listman Jr.*

Officers, No Fight!" that Croxton later on told a presidential commission inexplicably that there should be "one battalion officered by white men and one by negroes."[131]

Pressures to appoint white officers came from home and beyond. Many in the white community thought the higher-paying and more prestigious officer positions should only be assigned to white soldiers. In a letter published in the *Planet* nearly a month later, Major W.H. Johnson of the Second Battalion and the other officers who resigned with him presented their side of the story. By then, many very negative reports had appeared in the white press, presenting a most unfavorable view of the black officers. Johnson and his colleagues thus hoped to correct the record.

They started off by acknowledging that an act of Congress had indeed given commanding officers the authority to "ask for a Board to examine into the qualifications, efficiency, conduct and capability of officers under him." As they pointed out, however, that same authority gave an officer the means by which he could "get rid of any officers who may be objectionable to him, whether on account of color or anything else."[132]

The Second Battalion officers then provided an explanation for why they resigned, rather than undergo the examination. In effect, they felt that the process was predetermined. They argued that the board comprised officers who were negatively predisposed to the Sixth Virginia. Consequently, they suggested, the black officers could not possibly receive a fair hearing, no

# Richmond's Leigh Street Armory & African American Militia

Officers and NCOs of the Second Battalion, circa 1895. Virginia State University. "Seated in the center (*holding sword under chin*) is Major William H. Johnson, battalion commander. Standing behind him (*center*) is Captain John A.C. Stevens, commander of Company C, the 'Petersburg Blues.'" *Caption by John W. Listman Jr.*

matter who was appointed to the board. Their letter to the *Planet* elaborated on this point:

> *We were sent for. While some of us were standing at the front of the commanding officer's tent waiting for the others to appear, we heard the question coming from within the closed tent "Are there any officers or men fit for promotion?" The reply was "No." In a few minutes the President of the Board came out and said to us, "The Board will convene Wednesday, 5th, at 9 A.M.*
>
> *"If any of you wish to resign you had better do so before the Board meets. If your resignations are not in before we meet we'll have to report on you."*
>
> *The intention to get rid of colored officers was evident. We did not fear a fair examination as some of us had been examined more than once, and one of us three times, being always successful; but we were satisfied that it was a case of trot them out and knock them down.*[133]

The officers concluded their letter by expressing a transparent sense of hopelessness over the situation. Included was their suggestion that the commanding officer, Colonel Croxton, was at the center of a conspiracy to rid the Second Battalion of its black officers and replace them with white ones. They also pointed to the color consciousness of the white army officers generally and their racial disparagement of the black soldiers:

> *One thing has been demonstrated, yea two, first, that the commanding officer of the Sixth Virginia Regiment has no respect for a man or color, refined or vicious.*
>
> *All look alike to him. Second, that in the eyes of a certain class of army officers, an enlisted man, or an officer either if he be a colored officer is no more than a yellow dog.*[134]

They did not believe that all of the white officers shared such views but understood that such were too few in number to impact the decisions being made. The black officers expressed unreservedly their disappointment and sense of hopelessness over this deplorable situation:

> *We do not wish it understood that we were utterly friendless. We were certain that we had one and probably two officers on the Board who would have given us justice, but one of the other officers was from a regiment very closely allied to the Georgia Regiment which gave us more trouble than all Camp Poland combined, while the other two, one of whom was the President, was from*

Officers of the Second Battalion at Camp Poland, Tennessee, 1898. *Virginia State University.* "Major William H. Johnson is seated in front of his tent, just to the left. Taken in the autumn of 1898, Major Johnson commanded the 2nd Battalion, 6th Virginia. Since Johnson resigned and returned home on 15 October 1898, this image had to have been taken prior to that date. Note the enlisted man in the background with a .45 caliber Springfield rifle, used by almost all Guard troops (white and black) in the war." *Caption by John W. Listman Jr.*

Officers of the Sixth Virginia Volunteer Infantry at Camp Poland, Tennessee, 1898. *Virginia State University.* "This is probably just of the officers who served with the 2nd Battalion. It had to have been taken prior to his resignation and return to Petersburg on 15 October 1898, as it shows only black and none of the white replacement officers." *Caption by John W. Listman Jr.*

> *a regiment, the 4th Tennessee, who hated us intensely, as evidenced by their action on learning that we were to be temporarily assigned to the same brigade with them. We had nothing to hope for. Only swift judgment.*[135]

They were right about the swift judgment. Seeing no prospect for a fair resolution, the Second Battalion's resigned black officers demanded that they be mustered out of service. The government assented to their request, sending them home in October. Their time in service from that dramatic moment in October, when they learned of the inquiry into their qualifications, to their discharge from service was about a month. Despite Ham's heretofore rather benign reporting of camp life, it now seems clear that the Sixth Virginia soldiers had endured prejudice and humiliation from the beginning of their enlistment to the bitter end. The underlying conflicts appear to have ignited when they moved to the larger encampments and set up positions near the white regiments.

At the recommendation of Colonel Croxton and facing pressure from white constituents, Virginia's Governor Tyler appointed white officers to

take the place of the Second Battalion's black officers who had resigned their positions. As might be expected, the appointments very much upset the black soldiers, and they responded loudly and vigorously. At first, when the newly appointed white officers gave commands, the Second Battalion soldiers did not respond. Continued attempts to have their orders followed produced hoots, hisses and determined resistance. Camp officials assigned white regiments to surround the black troops in an attempt to persuade them to obey orders, but with little success. Even a speech by Major Johnson of the First Battalion did not help. The men ended their protest, however, when Colonel Croxton promised to take their grievance to the governor of Virginia, a promise that he failed to honor.[136]

Continued resistance, passive and otherwise, made it so difficult for the newly appointed white officers that they tendered their resignations after two weeks. The secretary of war, however, rejected these on the grounds that the appointment of replacements would only exacerbate the situation. So the Second Battalion of the Sixth Virginia continued from that point on with white officers; the First Battalion retained its original black officers.[137]

## The Conflicts Continue at Camp Haskell

In November, the troops got word that they were to be transferred south to Camp Haskell, located outside Macon, Georgia. Their removal to this camp further heightened anxieties over the climate of prejudice and hostility the black soldiers expected they would encounter in the Deep South. This only exacerbated the tensions among the already disillusioned soldiers of the Sixth Virginia. Ham's November 28 letter to the *Planet*, published in early December, commented on the exhausting and tedious twenty-hour train trip to Macon. He also spoke favorably of the general conditions of this new camp, noting, in particular, that other black regiments were stationed there. Importantly, the Tenth Regiment of Immunes was there, a black regiment that included a number of recruits from Richmond.

In preparing for the Spanish-American War, the military aggressively recruited southern troops to serve as "Immunes." They did this under the belief that men raised in the South, because their bodies were accustomed to hot and humid climates, would be more immune to tropical diseases than would other troops. They assumed that black soldiers would be especially well suited to cope with the health challenges commonly found in such tropical environs as Cuba. As should come as no surprise, these unsubstantiated assumptions did not prove to be valid during that war.[138]

Ironically, the racial conflicts drew the Immunes directly into the struggles involving the Sixth Virginia.[139] Ham wrote the following about the Immunes:

**Colored Volunteers Wanted.**

Eighty-two colored volunteers wanted for the 10th U. S. Volunteer Infantry commanded by Colonel Jesse M. Lee. This regiment is to have colored lieutenants for each company, and all non-commissioned officers are to be colored men.

Volunteers will be enrolled and mustered into service at 603 East Broad St., city, where the enrolling officer will be every day from 9 a. m. to 5 p. m. Board will be furnished recruits when necessary, while awaiting muster in.

CRANDAL MACKEY,
Capt. 10th U. S. Vol. Inf.

Ad recruiting "immunes"— "Colored Volunteers Wanted"—in the *Richmond Planet,* July 2, 1898, p. 1. *Library of Virginia.*

> Among the regiments stationed here are the Seventh and Tenth Regiments of Immunes and the Third North Carolina, with whom we were encamped at Knoxville. The other regiments here are the Second Ohio and the Third Engineers, both white. Among the Immune Regiment we have met several boys from Richmond, and they gave us a hearty greeting when our train rolled into camp. They have been encamped since August, and for a time were at Augusta, Ga., and then at Lexington, Kentucky, having reached Camp Haskell, only a few days ahead of us.[140]

Shortly after arriving in Camp Haskell, another major crisis arose within the Sixth Virginia, specifically within the Second Battalion, and this would have major consequences for the regiment as a whole. Some members of the Second Battalion became involved in two racial protests that ultimately would lead the army to muster the Sixth out of service. Historian Bruce A. Glasrud summarized the events as follows:

> *Several of the Virginians responded to white taunting by chopping down a persimmon tree that supposedly had been used to hang black men. Others tore down racist signs. In December, a streetcar conductor shot and killed an enlisted man of the 6th Virginia for not sitting in the black section of his trolley. Nevertheless, after allegedly threatening white townspeople, the entire regiment was arrested, disarmed, and placed under guard.*[141]

Ham reported that the camp leadership arrested the Sixth and used Tenth Immunes to guard them. Continuing to demoralize the men, the army also confiscated the regiment's weapons. Here is how Mitchell reported the precipitating incident:

> *Soon after arriving here someone pointed out to the boys a tree, on which a colored man, named Singleton was lynched several years ago. It was a large persimmon tree, and some of them got axes and cut it down. The owner was not troubled at all. The trouble about the park amounted to this. A few of them went into a park about half a mile from camp, that had little signs, tacked on the trees, "No niggers and dogs allowed in here." They got into a row with the park-keeper, and tore the signs down. A few of the men went to town with their guns, but none of them had cartridges, and they were arrested by the Provost Guard, and brought back to camp. Our camp was placed under arrest and the guns of the men taken away.*[142]

This being the second major conflict involving soldiers from the Sixth Virginia, the reaction to the violence very possibly was harsher than it might otherwise have been. Ham reported that camp officials placed the following additional restrictions on the soldiers:

> *Sunday morning, the 20th inst., since which time, no one has been allowed to go out or come into camp. Up to Wednesday we did not get our mail regularly, but now everything is working smoothly, and we have mail twice daily. As to any of our men being bucked and gagged, nothing of the kind*

*has ever been done, as the boys have not resisted arrest, and everything is perfectly quiet in camp.*[143]

Not having their guns available to them, the members of the Sixth Virginia spent their time beautifying their camp. Ham explained that "squad drills are held three times daily, and the fatigue details, which are very heavy, spend the day cleaning up, and straightening out the camp. In a few days this will be the most beautiful camp site in the neighborhood."[144] The reality of the humiliations inflicted on the troops clearly betrayed the latter attempt at dry humor. A similar betrayal of reality applies to Ham's upbeat focus on details as commonplace as the weather and changing conditions in camp: "The weather is beautiful here, in the daytime, sunshine and warm, but the nights are clear and cold. Many of the officers and men are using wood stoves, and have had their tents boarded up on the inside, and a good many of the tents are doubled with an opening in the center; which makes them more comfortable, and easier to be heated."[145]

The white officers asked the First Battalion's Major J.B. Johnson to round up the soldiers' arms, an order with which he complied. Johnson told the Sixth Virginia soldiers that because new Krag-Jorgensen rifles were about to be delivered, they should stack their older Springfield weapons. Ham's report suggests that the soldiers at the time were unaware of the hidden purpose behind this command, which, as it turned out, was to disarm the men without incident. Once that was done, white soldiers went through the camp confiscating all other possible weapons, including pocketknives, shears and razors. Then, camp leaders assigned the Tenth Regiment of Immunes to stand guard over the Sixth Virginia.[146]

Ham wrote that the new rifles carry "five balls in the magazine, and one in the chamber. They carry a ball of 30 caliber and are much lighter in weight than the old Springfield which we have been using." The Krag-Jorgensen rifle, a bolt-action long rifle, was developed originally in Norway. The military adopted it for use in the Spanish-American War. Because the rifles were in short supply at the time, the camp leadership did not immediately distribute them to all of the troops. The army never provided them to the Sixth Virginia prior to them being discharged from service. Interestingly, Ham did note that the army had already supplied the Immune Regiments (the Tenth being mostly black) with those rifles.[147]

Ham attempted to put a positive face on the situation facing the Sixth Virginia. He wrote, "The boys are all well and hearty, and take matters philosophically, believing that all of their troubles will be peaceably settled.

Out of the whole command not more than sixty were concerned in the rumpus anyhow."[148] His efforts, as with earlier reports, served more to reassure families and friends back home than to convey candidly what the troops were experiencing at camp.

## The Hope for Honor Remained

Continuing to be somewhat upbeat and not wanting to upset unduly those loved ones back home, Ham, a week later, tried not to convey the growing sense of hopefulness. Despite all that the black troops had experienced, he still focused on the possibility that they would be assigned to Cuba:

> *It is rumored that the time will expire in about 20 days and our pay for this month withheld for that length of time, but of course we know nothing official concerning this. The boys continue in their work as if nothing has happened, and at night they gather around their camp fires in the company streets, and each amuses himself according to his own inclination.*
>
> *It is a noticeable fact that while under arrest, the boys are cheerful and in good spirits. They have several good quartets, and their ringing voices can be heard from Mess call to Taps while the sweet strains of the different musical instruments are wafted on the breeze of these cold December nights. Every preparation is being made for an early departure for Cuba.*[149]

Perhaps intending to inject a bit of humor into what obviously were distressing circumstances, Ham wrote of a curious new secret organization that some of the soldiers had formed. Their razors and knives confiscated, the soldiers were unable to shave. So, some members of the Sixth Virginia formed what they called the Grand United Council of Uglies. This is how Ham described this council:

> *A unique and interesting secret organization has been formed in Camp, and takes the place of the Wednesday Club. It is known as the "grand United Council of Uglies." Ugliness is a prerequisite to membership, and every thing has to be done in an ugly manner by the ugly members, who are not at all superstitious, as the membership is limited to thirteen, and the meetings begin at thirteen minutes to seven and close at thirteen after eight every Friday.*[150]

Obviously, they needed a way to relieve the extraordinary stress as they wrestled with the incompatibilities between their role as soldiers and their ongoing struggles with race and military authority.

The discouragement and disappointments of the troops could not long be hidden. A soldier writing under the pseudonym "A. Blackman" wrote candidly about their situation, clarifying the perceived injustices perpetrated on the Sixth Virginia. In his report to the *Planet*, he expressed poignantly the sense of loss they were feeling for all they had sacrificed to serve their country and for the dashed hope that their loyalty and valor might go unnoticed. He wrote:

> *While the incarceration is only quasi, the men being allowed full liberty to anywhere within the camp limits and to the Y.M.C.A. tent, yet this is felt keenly by the men, many of whom gave up decent jobs, left comfortable homes and families, and sacrificed personal liberty in response to their country's call in her hour of sore distress and need.*
>
> *Notwithstanding the injustice of this arrest and the indignity and humiliation to which the men have been subjected, the more discreet among them keep up a cheerful air, and try to encourage the more despondent, so during the long evenings after the day's duties are done, at the blazing camp fires, tales are told, songs sung and for the time being all are oblivious to trouble.*[151]

One can only imagine how those back home reacted to what they read in the *Planet*. The soulfulness of this statement conveys unmistakably the emotions those men must have been experiencing. They had so hoped for gallant, patriotic service but were now undergoing a devastating humiliation at the hands of their camp's white officers.

By mid-December 1898, the troops got their rifles back—the old ones, not the new Krag-Jorgensen rifles—and camp leaders withdrew the Immunes from guarding them. Still, camp leaders restricted movements of Sixth Virginia troops in and out of camp.[152] In his report, Ham reflected the reality that their involvement in this now disheartening military adventure might soon come to an end. He wrote:

> *Many of the boys are putting in applications for furloughs home, during the holidays. Changes and incidents follow each other so rapidly in the affairs of this Command that it is unsafe to predict, or even think what will happen next. While seemingly everything points to a long campaign*

> in Cuba, and every preparation is being made therefore, currents flow to a probable early muster out.[153]

It is amazing that despite all, the members of the Sixth Virginia still held out hope that their service might continue. At the same time, they appeared resolved to what increasingly seemed inevitable, as Blackman observed in the foregoing, that an early muster out was impending. On December 13, 1898, Blackman wrote a stirring defense of the Sixth Virginia. First, he characterized the "indignity" and "cowardly incarceration" they had undergone in camp for twenty days. John Mitchell Jr. published it in the Christmas Eve edition of the *Planet*:

> Last Friday afternoon, after having been under arrest in quarters for twenty days, cut off from the outside world and for a portion of that time even deprived of the privilege of buying a newspaper or receiving our mail, the Sixth Virginia Regiment, U.S.V. Infantry was released from arrest. Was ever such an indignity ever perpetrated upon men who were brave and patriotic enough to offer their service to their country!…The true inwardness of this cowardly incarceration of more than eight hundred of Virginia's loyal sons will not be known until the Sixth Virginia is mustered out of service and the men and officers free to express their opinions and tell the real cause of the trouble in the regiment.[154]

Blackman also praised the *Planet* and, thus, editor Mitchell for the support provided through all they had endured: "We feel that the PLANET, ever champion of human rights and the defender of the oppressed, is the best medium to publish to the world the facts as they really exist."[155]

The inevitability of their pending discharge from service now appeared obvious. This was a time for reflection and for settling scores, so Blackman turned his fire on the regiment's commanding officer, Colonel Croxton, whom he blamed for all the Sixth had to endure:

> To begin with, Lieutenant-Colonel Croxton is the sole cause of all the trouble. Not being contented with his position and pay as a second lieutenant in the regular army, at the commencement of the unpleasantness between Spain and America, he sought promotion in the volunteer army. Being a Virginian, and having been detailed as military instructor in several of the military academies of the state, the surest means of elevation and promotion lay through the Virginia Volunteers.[156]

His critique then became still more targeted:

> *Peevish, fretful, and irascible by nature, he was more so, upon recovery from the sickness immediately preceding his taking command of the regiment. Knowing that he was an army officer, his harshness to both men and officers was from the first looked upon as a part of military discipline at first, and despite the oaths and general "cussing" for which the officers came in after every regimental parade, his will was law, and no one dared question it. This was at Camp Corbin. When he reached Knoxville, the same thing continued, and fault, nothing but fault was to be found, let the men do whatever they did.*[157]

In January 1899, the soldiers received word that their ordeal was about to end. They were to be mustered out and sent home. But one last affront lay ahead of them. Fearing further trouble from the Sixth Virginia, the War Department laid railroad tracks directly into Camp Haskell. This was to ensure that the hostile white community of Macon would not come into direct contact with the disillusioned soldiers.

Learning that each of the Sixth's soldiers had received his back pay, the local white merchants brought goods by wagon to the camp in hopes of extracting the departing soldiers' cash before they left for home. The soldiers did not take the bait, however, and left Camp Haskell with their funds intact. Families and friends happily greeted the Richmond contingent when they arrived at the city's Chesapeake and Ohio (C&O) train station. While surely comforted by this, those weary and disheartened men ended those nearly seven months not with the praise they had anticipated for having volunteered to serve their country. Instead, they carried with them painful memories of a prolonged struggle over equity and race, as well as the unfortunate label the press laid on them as the inglorious "Mutinous Sixth."[158]

The Tenth Regiment of Immunes, which in Macon had guarded the Sixth Virginia and was composed of black soldiers from Virginia and North Carolina, also faced racial conflicts in their relatively short period of service. The Tenth's return home from Camp Haskell was especially notable. Things did not go as peacefully for them as they had for the Sixth Virginia:

> *The regiment mustered out of service at Camp Haskell on March 8, 1899. After boarding trains, some of the soldiers fired their weapons and wounded a white teenager. By the time they reached Griffin, Georgia, the mayor had called up the local militia, the Griffin Rifles, to restore order. A*

Center canton of the regimental flag of the Sixth United States Colored Troops (USCT) from the Civil War. *Virginia State University*. "This image has no direct connection to the VA Guard, but belonged to Major William Henry Johnson of Petersburg. After its fall to Union forces in 1865, Petersburg was occupied by USCT units, including the 6th Regiment. According to the Virginia State University archivist, in 1987 the camp of the 6th USCT was near the boyhood home of Johnson. As a child, he apparently hung around the camp, interacting with the soldiers before the regiment was disbanded in 1866. Perhaps he was able to persuade Governor James Tyler to designate the newly organized black regiment as the 6th Virginia, after the 6th USCT regiment. Or, because three active duty white regiments were already designated 2nd, 3rd and 4th (the 1st was not mobilized at that time) and numerical precedence was very important, the option for a 5th Regiment might have been reserved so as to ensure that a black regiment would not be senior to it. However, one has to wonder why Johnson honored the image of the 6th USCT flag by fitting it into a cameo frame." *Caption by John W. Listman Jr.*

Muster out roll showing the names of Major Joseph B. Johnson as well as his white nemesis, white regiment officer Colonel Richard C. Croxton. *Library of Virginia.*

> *white brakeman was killed when either the militia or town citizens fired a volley into the train. At least one white Immune regiment, the 6th US Volunteers, exhibited similar behavior after discharge as the black 10th, but without a similar response. Regardless, other incidents occurred as the train delivered the soldiers to their homes: the Immunes were alleged to have shot off rounds, stolen whiskey, and looted saloons. They arrived in Richmond on March 10.*[159]

Thus ended a true bittersweet moment in American military history. This all occurred only three decades after African Americans received the rights and protections of citizenship promised by the Fourteenth Amendment. Almost nothing could more symbolically have expressed the hope for the exercise of full citizenship than being given the opportunity to carry weapons and fight in the service of their country. But those unfortunate racial confrontations while at camp conveyed unmistakably to the African American volunteers, their families and their friends the stark reality of the country's continuing and growing racial divide.

Those interracial conflicts and their subsequent waves of resistance were simply unprecedented in United States military history, in both their seriousness and consequences. This makes the courage and patriotism these soldiers and their officers displayed all the more remarkable, especially when viewed in the context of endemic prejudice and segregation.

CHAPTER 5

# A Light Shines in the Darkness

## *The Armory Lives On*

The Sixth Virginia's involvement in racial conflicts during the Spanish-American War did much to harden attitudes within the white community, throughout the South and nationally. Most governors across the country excluded black companies when they reorganized their militia units at the turn of the century, as did Virginia's Governor Tyler in the spring of 1899. A few years later, the United States Congress passed the Efficiency in Militia Act of 1903, known popularly as the Dick Act. This precipitated the conversion of America's militias into the National Guard, which formed officially in 1916, the year before the United States was drawn into World War I. From 1899 and for another sixty-five years—from 1899 to 1964—Virginia's National Guard admitted no African Americans. Other states admitted very few.[160]

### THE ARMORY BECOMES A SCHOOL

Adding insult to injury for Richmond's First Battalion, the Richmond School Board requested the city convert the Armory into a school—at the very same time the soldiers were returning home. This provided yet another unmistakable sign that the era of Virginia's black militia was over. The Richmond School Board's minutes recorded the reappropriation of that noble building: "On motion, the Committee on Buildings & Furniture was requested to petition the City Council for use of the Colored Armory building to be used as a school building in place of those now rented for Brook School."[161]

A month later, Richmond City Council offered and approved the following resolution:

> *Be it resolved by the Council of the City of Richmond the Board of alderman concurring that the Committee on Grounds and Buildings be and these are hereby authorized to allow the School Board to occupy temporarily the Colored Armory Building. Situated at the N.E. Corner of Leigh and St. Peter Streets for school purposes, in order to accommodate the Colored children, provided said School Board shall assume the expense of a janitor, gas, water, cleaning and heating said building, and of having such repairs made during the time of occupancy as may be necessary: and provided further that when notified to do so by the Committee on Grounds and Buildings, the said School Board shall turn the building back to the Committee and Grounds and Buildings and in the same condition it was at the time of occupation by the School Board.*[162]

It is interesting that city council's authorization to use the Armory was not a permanent one. The temporary assignment suggests that the council might have been uncertain about the First Battalion's future in the very days they were returning home.

The school board accepted city council's resolution regarding the Armory shortly thereafter, "subject to conditions prescribed in the resolution" that the council had approved and the mayor had accepted on March 18, 1899. Finally, the school board's annual report for the year ending July 31, 1899, specified that the students from the Brook School now attend school in what was to become the Monroe School for elementary children, in honor of former president James Monroe. Apparently, the board believed the building was highly suited for educational purposes and, in the city's judgment, only required minimal modifications. It also specified that in the upcoming session, the students then being taught on the grounds of the Moore Industrial School as well as the Brook School should occupy the Armory.[163]

And so, the Leigh Street building's role as an armory came to an abrupt conclusion. On the other hand, this did not end its special place in Richmond's African American community. For about eighty years more, that building served as a school for black children. From 1899 to 1940 and again from the end of World War II until 1981, it served as the home for a succession of schools, both primary and secondary.

In 1942, the Office of Civilian Defense (OCD) renovated the Armory to serve as a recreation center where black soldiers could rest and recuperate. The OCD also built a gymnasium to the rear of the building, which after the war the schools that acquired the Armory used as a gymnasium. By then, the former Monroe School building had become the Monroe Center.[164] In his application to place the building in the historical register, Selden Richardson quoted a newspaper article that described the remodeling the OCD had done:

> *When the remodeling is completed there will be on the first, beside the auditorium, a recreation room, a lounge room, an up-to-date kitchen, and a ladies' lounge room.*
>
> *Upstairs there is space enough for 100 cots and one of the smaller rooms on this floor is being turned into a shower room....This center is a beehive of activity most of the time as the building is the headquarters for Negro defense work in Richmond.*[165]

The National Park Service description of the Leigh Street Armory pointed out that some "56,000 soldiers passed through the building during this period."[166]

During World War II, the Office of Civilian Defense (OCD) converted the then Monroe Center into a service center for black soldiers. The gymnasium that the OCD built is to the rear of the building. *Library of Virginia.*

Volunteers to help at the Monroe Center during World War II, circa 1942. *Afro-American Newspapers Archives and Research Center (AANARC)*.

Soldiers relaxing in the Monroe Center during World War II, circa 1942. *AANARC*.

Soldiers playing pool in the Monroe Center during World War II, circa 1942. *AANARC.*

Following World War II, Armstrong High School, located conveniently across the street, used the Monroe Center as its annex until 1952. The building provided overflow classrooms, offices, storage space and, importantly, a gymnasium. After Armstrong High School moved to its new building east of Richmond, the Armory served as the Colored Special School, a school for students with particular health and functional issues, from 1952 to 1954. Having taken over the old Armstrong High School, Graves Middle School acquired and began using the Armory building in 1955. It, too, used the Armory as an annex and a gymnasium from 1955 to 1981.[167]

After the building ceased functioning as a school in 1981, the newly established Virginia Museum for Black History and Archives, Inc. began making plans to establish the historic Armory as a museum. In 1983, the museum announced plans to raise money to renovate the Armory, and in March 1985, Carroll Anderson Sr., then president of the museum's board of directors, officially announced a fundraising campaign to raise just over $2 million for renovations and operations. However, while the building served for a brief time as the projected home for the museum, a major fire and a lack of funds forced the organization to give up on its renovation plans. In his application to have the Armory placed in the National Register of Historic Places, Selden Richardson noted that also that year and before the museum moved in, a "fire damaged the roof and upper floors of the building. After this fire, the damaged roof and second floor were not repaired, the Black History Museum moved to other facilities, and the armory has been vacant since then." The museum moved three blocks away to what was then known as the Adolf Dill home at 00 Clay Street. There it stayed for just over thirty years and, while there, changed its name to the Black History Museum and Cultural Center of Virginia.[168]

In that same time period, the Armory passed through a very uncertain period. Richmond officials left the building largely unattended and subject to the deteriorating effects of weather and time. The city did, however, play a key role in deflecting efforts to convert the building to private use or to come under the wrecking ball of progress. According to Richardson, the city designated the Armory as surplus property. In 2002, grant funds from

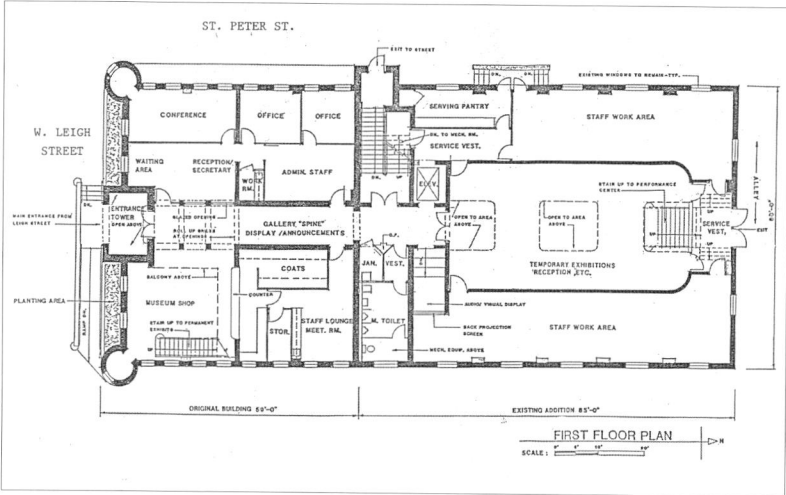

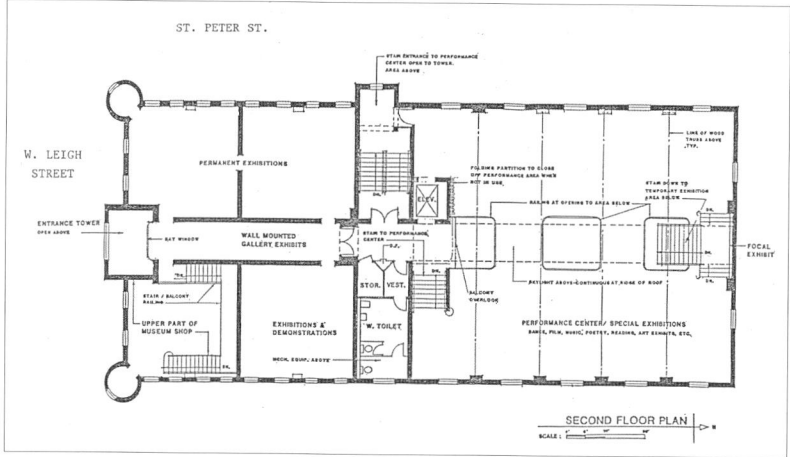

Architectural plans for the Monroe Center, 1985. *Black History Museum and Cultural Center of Virginia.*

Inside gymnasium in poor condition before demolition, circa 2000. *Selden Richardson*.

Gymnasium demolition underway, 1998. *Selden Richardson*.

the U.S. Department of the Interior's "Save America's Treasures" program provided the monies needed to stabilize the building. In his proposal to place the Armory in the National Register of Historic Places, Richardson wrote that the renovations involved removing deteriorated wood structures and stabilizing the masonry. He said that the project involved removing the roof and most interior woodwork and almost all of the interior woodwork, ceilings and floors. Renovations also reworked the signature crenellated features of the roofline and chimneys. The city stabilized the roof and installed new joists and floors.[169]

In 2010, leadership from the Black History Museum took a renewed interest in the Armory. They learned that the city might be willing to sell it to the museum on favorable terms. After carefully considering the costs of renovating and moving to the Armory, as well as the need to preserve this historically significant building, the museum initiated a major fundraising and renovation effort focused on restoring the building and converting it into a museum and cultural center for the city of Richmond and the commonwealth of Virginia.

This time, the development effort was a success, and the Armory reemerged on May 5, 2016, as the new home of the Black History Museum and Cultural Center of Virginia. The Armory thus once again became a

Second-floor ceiling and roof damage from the fire, 2002. *Selden Richardson.*

*Left*: The fire did extensive damage to the building, 2002. *Selden Richardson.*

*Below*: More damage from the fire, 2002. *Selden Richardson.*

*Left*: Note the tin ceiling tiles that were in the building at the time of the fire, 2002. *Selden Richardson*.

*Below*: Partial restoration and stabilization of roof and ceiling joists, 2002. *Selden Richardson*.

Partial restoration and stabilization of turret, 2002. *Selden Richardson.*

Structure for supporting a flagpole can be seen in the center of the front square turret, 2002. *Selden Richardson.*

Renovated Armory at night, 2016. *Ansel Olson (photographer).*

The museum's 2013 rendering of anticipated changes to the Armory. Burt Pinnock was the architect. *Black History Museum and Cultural Center of Virginia.*

majestic and powerful symbol of community pride. In this iteration, the Armory is now a place where the history and culture African Americans helped make in Virginia can be preserved, presented and advanced.

Editor John Mitchell Jr., Major Joseph B. Johnson, Colonel Wilfred Emory Cutshaw and many others involved in the Armory's founding undoubtedly would be pleased if they knew that their efforts to create something of such great worth had survived. Were they to see that building today, surely they would say, as did Mitchell in 1895, that the "beautifully lighted armory" can once again "be seen from this section glowing in magnificent splendor."

## More Than a Building

The very brevity of its service as the headquarters for an African American militia—lasting just over three years—does little to diminish the Leigh Street Armory's historic significance to Richmond, Virginia, or the nation. This is for a number of reasons.

First, as an unlikely architectural and historical survivor, it has become an authentic yet silent reminder of America's ongoing struggle with race and race relations. City officials built the Leigh Street Armory exactly three decades after the Civil War ended slavery, when the nation's tentative experiment with African American freedom and citizenship was in its earliest stages. Now, in the second decade of the twenty-first century, the Armory's renovation and repurposing comes in the midst of yet another transition in the country's struggles over race, as the nation addresses the inequities and imperfections inherent in its more than fifty-year-old investment in expanded civil rights. The Armory's continued presence, thus, in many ways, serves as a reminder of how far the United States has come and has yet to travel as it seeks to narrow its gnawing and persistent racial divide.

Second, the irony cannot be overstated that Richmond, Virginia, was the only city in America to build a free-standing, nineteenth-century armory for the exclusive use of black militia soldiers. On the other hand, Virginia was the leading force in framing a constitution that incorporated slavery into the nation's legal structures, the lead importer from Africa of enslaved persons to America, the unrivaled "wholesaler" of enslaved persons across the nation, the one southern state that allowed its largest city to serve as the capital for the Confederate States of America and, by the time of the Armory's construction, a lead participant in launching the extended period of institutionalized racial segregation.

Of course, that building did not come to be merely by chance. As demonstrated in this study, a number of factors contributed to the city's decision to build it. Two were especially important: Virginia's black militia soldiers served faithfully and effectively in the Virginia Volunteers for more than twenty years prior to the Armory's construction; and key black political and militia leaders worked tirelessly and successfully to persuade the white-dominated Richmond City Council to agree to move the project forward.

Third, the very survival of that building, after nearly a century and a quarter of misuse and inattention, is testament to the need for all Americans to be vigilant about preserving even the most seemingly unremarkable of community relics. Such hidden treasures often provide some of the clearest lenses through which to peer at times long past and learn lessons of enormous value for the future. Surely, preservation of the historic Leigh Street Armory has brought to light one of the most interesting and unique examples of African Americans striving to gain the rights that the end of slavery had promised.

Fourth, the active role the militias played in the late eighteenth and nineteenth centuries is a specific reminder of a military yesteryear, of the country's early efforts to balance the virtues of a standing army against the idealized image of homegrown, volunteer militias. Their study helps us discern what the founders might have been thinking when they inserted that now rather archaic word "militia" into both the original U.S. Constitution and the subsequent Bill of Rights

Fifth, the remaining armories from that era point out a very challenging time in American history—the Gilded Age. In those years, cities used militias to quell civil unrest, most especially those that widespread prejudices and economic disparities had produced. The proud militias and their stately armories thus provide visible reminders of that turbulent history. They help Americans understand how in addressing societal conflicts, the nation can easily overlook the underlying unfairness and consequent social dislocations that contributed to the conflicts in the first place.

Finally, the militias and armories of the late nineteenth century speak volumes about how in the past Americans expressed a sense of community, patriotism and honor. The gallantly dressed and precisely disciplined militias were often central to America's national, state and city celebrations and sense of patriotism. Their armories were massive and impressive symbols of that centrality as well. Such was uniquely meaningful for late nineteenth-century African Americans who derived from the black militias—and, in the case of Richmond, also from the Leigh Street Armory—the hope that in America all men truly are created equal.

APPENDIX

# The Armory Before and After Renovation

*Photographs by Karl Elchinger*

Photographs Pre-Renovation (2014), pages 131–137

Photographs Post-Renovation (2016), pages 138–142

Front of the Armory, looking northeast. In the 2002 preservation and stabilization project, funded with a Save America's Treasures grant, the glass windows were removed, stored and replaced by temporary wood windows. They were painted to look like glass windows.

# Appendix

A close-up of the front gate.

The deteriorating original front gate.

# Appendix

A close-up of deteriorating wood and brick structures inside the building.

Looking from the back west side room through the door into the front west side room. Remnants of blackboards can be seen on the wall. Blackboards were installed in most of the rooms in the years the Armory functioned as a school.

# Appendix

West wall in the back hall on the second floor. The exit marker on the wall points to where the top of the stairs was located (placed there in the years following World War II).

Large second-floor east room, looking south. The entry to the southeast turret can be seen to the left.

# Appendix

The back hall looking to the east. This space, which was constructed in the 1942 renovation, served as a divider between the Armory and the gymnasium that the black GIs had used during World War II. The holes in the floor to the right were likely installed for showers. The building's original windows can be seen stacked in this space (placed there in 2002). The wall to the right was originally the outside back wall of the Armory; its having been converted to an inside wall accounts for the plaster on the wall.

Front southwest corner on the second floor. The entry to the round turret is in the center of the image.

# Appendix

The main hall on the second floor, looking from back to front. One can see the bricked-in door on the left just inside the hall. The brick visible on the outside of the entryway was originally the outside back wall of the Armory. This doorway into the hall also was original. It opened onto a back deck that had been installed off the second floor.

# Appendix

The back room on the west side looking to the back (north). Blackboard remnants can be seen on the walls.

A close-up of the interior of a round turret. Coat hanging braces (probably installed in the years the building served as a school) are on the sides of the turret wall. The turret door frame and the vents installed at the bottom of the temporary wood window are visible.

# Appendix

# Appendix

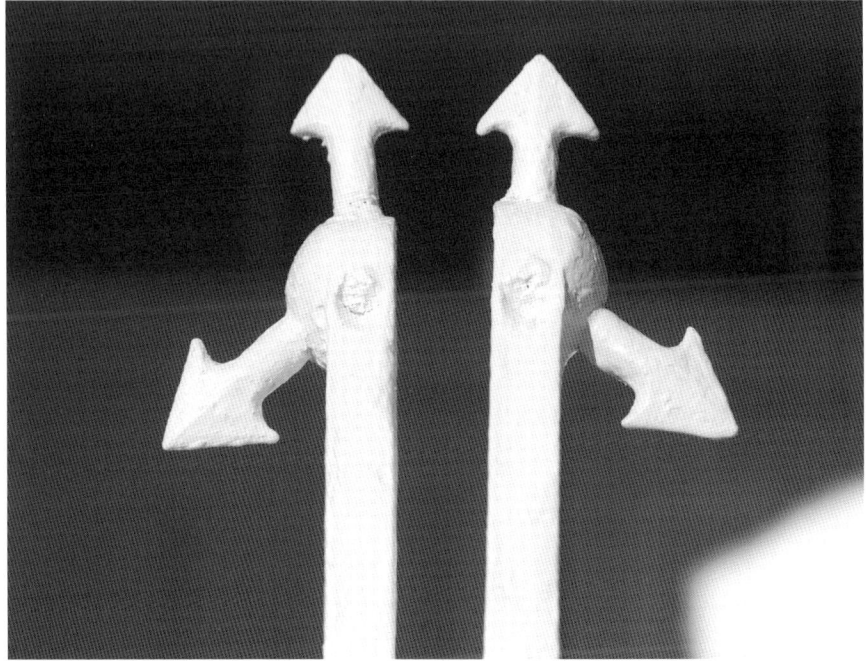

*This page, top*: The new museum sign.

*This page, bottom*: The top spikes of the front gate.

*Opposite*: Southwest corner of the Armory.

# Appendix

Close-up of the refurbished front gate.

# Appendix

*Right*: Refurbished front door.

*Below*: Back room on the west side of the first floor looking through doors into the front west side room. The door to the right was added as part of the renovations.

# Appendix

Second-floor wall that originally was on the back outside of the Armory. This image shows the new glass door and renovated central hallway. The wall behind the piano, the original outside back wall of the Armory, became an inside wall in the hall when the gymnasium was built. The gymnasium was torn down in 1998, but that back hall remained until the museum renovated the building as part of the 2014–16 renovation and restoration project. The new addition begins where the hall once was located.

Renovated upstairs room in the Armory, showing refurbished blackboards and reflections from windows.

# Notes

## Chapter 1

1. See Galvin, *Minute Men*; Gross, *Minutemen and Their World*; and U.S. Army War College, *Examination of George Washington*.
2. Glasrud, "African American Militia Units in Virginia."
3. Washington, "On Recruiting and Maintaining an Army."
4. Library of Congress, *Acts of the Second Congress*.
5. Hening, *Hening's Statutes at Large*, 226.
6. See James' classic *Black Jacobins*; Schwarz, *Gabriel's Conspiracy*; Breen, *Land Shall Be Deluged*; and Horwitz, *Midnight Rising*.
7. See Berlin, Reidy and Rowland, *Freedom's Soldiers*.
8. Robert C. Kennedy, "On This Day: The Freedmen's Bureau (*Harper's Weekly*, July 25, 1868)," HarpWeek, 2001, www.nytimes.com/learning/general/onthisday/harp/0725.html.
9. Halbrook, *Freedmen, the Fourteenth*, 17.
10. Cunningham, "'They Are Proud of Their Uniforms,'" 34.
11. Ibid.
12. Ibid., 42. For an exploration of African American laborers, see Rachleff, *Black Labor in Richmond*.
13. Glasrud, "African American Militia Units in Virginia."
14. Ibid.
15. Cunningham, "'They Are Proud of Their Uniforms,'" 42.
16. John Listman to Roice Luke, 2017.

17. Alexander, "No Officers, No Fight!," 169.
18. Ibid.
19. Cunningham, "'They Are Proud of Their Uniforms,'" 52.
20. Glasrud, "African American Militia Units in Virginia," 2015.
21. "Who Goes There?—Newport News in Possession of the Richmond Military," *Richmond Dispatch*, January 13, 1887.
22. Cunningham, "'They Are Proud of Their Uniforms,'" 53.
23. "Convicts in Peril—A Fire at the Penitentiary at 5:30 A.M. Threatens 800 Lives," *Richmond Dispatch*, February 1, 1888.
24. "A Gala Day—The Parade a Success—Fully 5000 in Line and Two Miles in Length," *Richmond Planet*, October 18, 1890.
25. Ibid.
26. Ibid.
27. John Listman to Roice Luke, 2017.
28. "A Gala Day," *Richmond Planet*, October 18, 1890.
29. Ibid.
30. Ibid. Reverend W.W. Browne was William Washington Browne, member of the black fraternal organization the Grand Fountain of the United Order of True Reformers and founder of the True Reformers bank in Richmond. Virginia Normal and Collegiate Institute is now Virginia State University.
31. "President Hayes Speaks—The Emancipation Celebration—A Brilliant Street Parade," *Richmond Planet*, January 8, 1898.
32. Ibid.
33. Ibid.
34. Ibid.
35. Ibid.
36. Ibid.
37. "Colored Troops on the March—They Celebrate Their Anniversary—A Military Pageant," *Richmond Planet*, June 18, 1898.

# *Chapter 2*

38. According to the Economic History Association via MeasuringWorth.com, the $600,000 price tag of the New York City Seventh Regiment Armory would be approximately $13.2 million (2016). The $10,000 spent on the Leigh Street Armory in Richmond would be approximately $259,000 (2016).

39. Fogelson, *America's Armories*, chapter 4.
40. Twain and Warner, *Gilded Age*.
41. Richardson, "Reconstructing the Gilded Age," 7.
42. Tipple, "Anatomy of Prejudice," 510, 521.
43. Zinn, *People's History of the United States*, 245–51; Brecher, "Great Upheaval of 1877."
44. Green, *Death in the Haymarket*.
45. Fogelson, *America's Armories*, 41.
46. Authors' conclusion.
47. See Amar, *America's Constitution*.
48. Franklin and Higginbotham, *From Slavery to Freedom*, 105.
49. See Deyle, *Carry Me Back*, 142–63. For analysis of the visual specter of the domestic trade in Virginia, see McInnis, *Slaves Waiting for Sale*. See also McInnis, "Mapping the Slave Trade in Richmond," 102–25; and Heier, "Accounting for the Business of Suffering," 60–83.
50. See Lankford, *Richmond Burning*.
51. "The New Armory—Richmond's Gift to Its Soldiery," *Richmond Planet*, December 21, 1895; Library of Congress, Chronicling America, chroniclingamerica.loc.gov/lccn/sn84025841/1895-12-21/ed-1/seq-1, accessed July 18, 2017.
52. Cunningham, "'They Are Proud of Their Uniforms,'" 34–35, 42.
53. Ibid., 43.
54. Ibid., 50.
55. Ibid., 36.
56. "New Armory," *Richmond Planet*, December 21, 1895.
57. "Richmond, Va., City Council—Jackson Ward's Representatives," *Richmond Planet*, February 16, 1895.
58. Richardson, National Register of Historic Places Registration Form, First Battalion Virginia Volunteer Armory, 2009.

# Chapter 3

59. "New Armory," *Richmond Planet*, December 21, 1895.
60. Ibid.
61. Ibid.
62. Ibid.
63. *Daily Times* (Richmond, VA), September 8, 1886; January 17, 1888; January 27, 1888; Library of Congress, Chronicling America.

64. *Richmond Dispatch*, September 4, 1888; "New Armory," *Richmond Planet*, December 21, 1895.
65. $7,500 Is the Amount—An Armory for the Colored Troops," *Richmond Planet*, January 6, 1894.
66. Ibid.
67. "New Armory," *Richmond Planet*, December 21, 1895.
68. Ibid.
69. Ibid.
70. Ibid.
71. We are fortunate that the Library of Virginia has preserved many editions of Mitchell's newspaper, microfilm copies of which are available onsite at the library, as well as through the Library of Congress's searchable online site, Chronicling America. This is important not only because Mitchell published local, regional and national stories of interest to African Americans but also, as was common for many newspaper editors at that time, he wrote a lot about himself. Mitchell played prominent roles in so many aspects of Richmond's and Virginia's African American community in the late 1800s and early 1900s, and as a consequence, he preserved a history that otherwise would today be largely unknown.
72. "Armory for the Colored People," *Richmond Planet*, July 7, 1894.
73. "A Mayor's Peculiar Veto—Assigns Color for the Reason for His Action—The Board Acts Promptly," *Richmond Planet*, October 13, 1894.
74. *Alexandria Gazette and Virginia Advertiser*, October 11, 1894, Library of Congress, Chronicling America.
75. "A Mayor's Peculiar Veto," *Richmond Planet*, October 13, 1894.
76. Ibid.
77. "New Armory," *Richmond Planet*, December 21, 1895.
78. "New Howitzer Home—The Handsome Armory Building to Be Formally Opened Next Week," *Richmond Dispatch*, March 24, 1895.
79. Ibid.
80. *Richmond Times-Dispatch*, January 18, 1913, 8.
81. "White Brick-Layers—They Protest Against Colored Workmen," *Richmond Planet*, March 9, 1895.
82. Ibid.
83. Ibid.
84. Ibid.
85. Ibid.
86. Alexander, *Race Man*, 40–59, 71–88.

87. For example, see "Editor Mitchell Travels," *Richmond Planet*, November 27, 19210.
88. Alexander, *Race Man*, see chapters 4, 10, 11 and 12.
89. Ibid., 185–204.
90. "New Armory," *Richmond Planet*, December 21, 1895.
91. Ibid.
92. Ibid.
93. Ibid.
94. Ibid.
95. Department of the Interior, National Park Service, "Byrd Park Pump House," www.nps.gov/nr/travel/richmond/ByrdParkPumpHouse.html, accessed July 17, 2017.
96. Richardson Application, United States Department of the Interior/National Park Service, National Register of Historic Places Registration Form, First Battalion Virginia Volunteer Armory, 2009, www.dhr.virginia.gov/registers/cities/richmond/127-5676_leigh_street_armory_2009_nr_final.pdf
97. "New Armory," *Richmond Planet*, December 21, 1895.
98. "Our City Engineer—An Honored Official," *Richmond Planet*, January 11, 1896. The front page of the *Planet* published a large photo of Cutshaw in conjunction with the article.
99. "The Colored Armory—Major Johnson Received the Handsome Structure," *Richmond Planet*, October 12, 1895.
100. Ibid. The original Armory did indeed have a two-story balcony on the back side of the building that overlooked the area where the troops often drilled. It is possible that when the Office of Civilian Defense in 1942 converted the Armory into a World War II service center for black soldiers, it demolished the balcony to make room for a new gym planned for the rear of the building. Or, the city could already have demolished it in the years the Armory served as an elementary school.
101. "The Colored Armory," *Richmond Planet*, October 12, 1895.
102. Ibid.
103. Ibid.
104. "Jackson Ward Brevities," *Richmond Planet*, October 19, 1895.
105. "The New Colored Armory—The Handsome Structure Will Be Finished Within Ten Days—It Is a Most Creditable Building," *Times* (Richmond, VA), September 8, 1895.
106. "New Armory—St. Peter & Leigh Sts—Military Bazaar," *Richmond Planet*, October 12, 1895; October 19, 1895; October 26, 1895.

107. "The Colored Armory," *Richmond Planet*, December 21, 1895.
108. Ibid.

## Chapter 4

109. Louis Fisher, "Destruction of the *Maine* (1898)," April 4, 2009, Law Library of Congress, Library of Congress, www.loc.gov/law/help/usconlaw/pdf/Maine.1898.pdf, accessed August 4, 2017.
110. "The Eagles Criticism," *Richmond Planet*, May 28, 1898.
111. *Richmond Planet*, May 28, 1898.
112. "Frivolous Reasons," *Richmond Planet*, June 11, 1898.
113. Alexander, "No Officers, No Fight!," 159–71.
114. "Governor Tyler Refuses to Remove Colored Officers," *Richmond Planet*, June 18, 1898.
115. Ibid.
116. "Colored Troops for the Army—Larger Numbers Examined—Many Rejected," *Richmond Planet*, July 2, 1898.
117. Ibid.
118. Ibid.
119. Alexander, "No Officers, No Fight!," page 58.
120. "The War Department and Colored Officers—A Letter to the Secretary of War—The Assistant Adjutant General Makes Reply," *Richmond Planet*, July 9, 1898.
121. Ibid.
122. "The Colored Troops in Camp," *Richmond Planet*, July 30, 1898.
123. "Camp Corbin News—Six Companies in Camp," *Richmond Planet*, August 6, 1898.
124. "Camp Corbin News—Eight Companies in Camp," *Richmond Planet*, August 13, 1898.
125. Ibid.
126. "The Last Camp Corbin Notes—A Shadow of the Past," *Richmond Planet*, September 17, 1898.
127. "Camp Poland Notes—Change of Location," *Richmond Planet*, October 1, 1898.
128. "Camp Poland Notes—Division Review—Sixth Regiment in Fine Shape," *Richmond Planet*, September 24, 1898; "Camp Poland Notes," *Richmond Planet*, October 1, 1898.
129. "Colored Officers Resign," *Richmond Planet*, October 8, 1898.
130. "Trouble in the 6th Virginia," *Richmond Planet*, October 15, 1898.

131. Alexander, "No Officers, No Fight!"
132. "The Silence Broken!—Colored Officers of the Sixth Virginia Tell the Whole Story," *Richmond Planet*, November 19, 1898.
133. Ibid.
134. Ibid.
135. Ibid.
136. "The Plot Is Foiled—Sixth Regiment Refuses to Obey Croxton's White Officers," *Richmond Planet*, November 5, 1898.
137. "Sixth Virginia Restless," *Richmond Planet*, November 12, 1898; "The Silence Broken!," *Richmond Planet*, November 19, 1898.
138. Cunningham, "We Are an Orderly Body of Men," 1.
139. "Camp Life of Virginians—A Cheering Letter from the Scenes of the Disturbance," *Richmond Planet*, December 3, 1898, 1.
140. Ibid.
141. Glasrud, "African American Militia Units in Virginia."
142. "Camp Life of Virginians," *Richmond Planet*, December 3, 1898.
143. Ibid.
144. Ibid.
145. Ibid.
146. Ibid.
147. Ibid.; "The Krag-Jorgensen Gun," *New York Times*, August 16, 1898.
148. "Camp Life of Virginians," *Richmond Planet*, December 3, 1898.
149. "Under Arrest at Macon, GA.—Condition of the Sixth Virginia," *Richmond Planet*, December 10, 1898.
150. Ham went on to list the members of the Ugly Club; members included the Ugly Grand Chaplain, the Ugly Historian and even "Ugly Ham Carter," perhaps shining light on Ham's identity. "Under Arrest at Macon, GA," *Richmond Planet*, December 10, 1898.
151. Ibid.
152. "Got Their Guns Back—Sixth Virginia on Dress Parade," *Richmond Planet*, December 17, 1898.
153. Ibid.
154. "Hard Times in the Sixth Virginia—A Peculiar Condition," *Richmond Planet*, December 24, 1898.
155. Ibid.
156. Ibid.
157. Ibid.
158. Alexander, "No Officers, No Fight!," 169–70.
159. Glasrud, "African American Militia Units in Virginia."

## Chapter 5

160. Listman, "Proud to Serve," 17.
161. Richmond School Board, Minutes of Committee on Buildings and Furniture, February 1899, City of Richmond archives, Old City Hall, Richmond, Virginia.
162. Richmond School Board, Minutes of Committee on Buildings and Furniture, March 18, 1899, City of Richmond archives, Old City Hall, Richmond, Virginia.
163. "Monroe School, RPS: A Mini History: Bits & Pieces," Richmond Public Schools, accessed July 31, 2017, web.richmond.k12.va.us/AboutRPSHistory/FN/Monroe.aspx.
164. Ibid.
165. Richardson, National Register of Historic Places Registration Form, First Battalion Virginia Volunteer Armory, 2009.
166. "Leigh Street Armory," National Park Service, www.nps.gov/nr/travel/richmond/FirstBattalionArmory.html.
167. Richardson, National Register of Historic Places Registration Form, First Battalion Virginia Volunteer Armory, 2009.
168. Ibid.
169. Ibid.

# Bibliography

## Newspapers

*Alexandria Gazette*
*New York Times*
*Richmond Dispatch*
*Richmond Planet*
*Richmond Times*
*Richmond Times-Dispatch*

## Published Works

Alexander, Ann Field. "No Officers, No Fight!" In *Brothers to the Buffalo Soldiers: Perspectives on the African American Militia and Volunteers, 1865–1917*, edited by Bruce A. Glasrud. Columbia: University of Missouri Press, 2011.

———. *Race Man: The Rise and Fall of the "Fighting Editor," John Mitchell Jr.* Charlottesville: University of Virginia Press, 2002.

Amar, Akhil Reed. *America's Constitution: A Biography*. New York: Random House, 2006.

Berlin, Ira, Joseph P. Reidy and Leslie S. Rowland, eds. *Freedom's Soldiers: The Black Military Experience in the Civil War*. Cambridge, UK: Cambridge University Press, 1998.

Brecher, Jeremy. "The Great Upheaval of 1877." Libcom.org. May 23, 2013. libcom.org/history/great-upheaval-1877-jeremy-brecher.

# Bibliography

Breen, Patrick. *The Land Shall Be Deluged with Blood: A New History of the Nat Turner Revolt*. New York: Oxford University Press, 2016.

Buckley, Gail. *American Patriots: The Story of Blacks in the Military from the Revolution to Desert Storm*. New York: Random House, 2001.

Burrs, Stacy L., and Roice D. Luke. "Richmond's First in the Nation Historic Building." *Richmond Times Dispatch*, September 16, 2012.

Clark, Kathleen Ann. *Defining Moments: African American Commemoration and Political Culture in the South 1863–1913*. Chapel Hill: University of North Carolina Press, 2006.

Cunningham, Roger D. "'They Are Proud of Their Uniforms as Any Who Serve Virginia': African American Participation in the Virginia Volunteers, 1872–1899." In *Brothers to the Buffalo Soldiers: Perspectives on the African American Militia and Volunteers, 1865–1917*, edited by Bruce A. Glasrud, 34–72. Columbia: University of Missouri Press, 2011.

———. "We Are an Orderly Body of Men: Virginia's Black 'Immunes' in the Spanish-American War." *Historic Alexandria Quarterly* (Summer 2001): 1. alexandriava.gov/uploadedfiles/historic/haw/HistoricAlexandriaQuarterly2001Summer.pdf.

Deyle, Steven. *Carry Me Back: The Domestic Slave Trade in American Life*. New York: Oxford University Press, 2005.

Edgerton, Robert B. *Hidden Heroism: Black Soldiers in America's Wars*. Boulder, CO: Westview Press, 2001.

Fogelson, Robert M. *America's Armories: Architecture, Society, and Public Order*. Cambridge, MA: Harvard University Press, 1989.

Franklin, John Hope, and Evelyn Brooks Higginbotham. *From Slavery to Freedom: A History of African Americans*. 9th ed. New York: McGraw-Hill, 2011.

Galvin, John R. *The Minute Men: The First Fight: Myths and Realities of the American Revolution*. Dulles, VA: Brassey's, 1996.

Glasrud, Bruce A. "African American Militia Units in Virginia (1870–1899)." In *Encyclopedia Virginia*, Virginia Foundation for the Humanities in partnership with the Library of Virginia, 2015. www.encyclopediavirginia.org/African_American_Militia_Units_in_Virginia_1870-1899.

———, ed. *Brothers to the Buffalo Soldiers: Perspectives on the African American Militia and Volunteers, 1865–1917*. Columbia: University of Missouri Press, 2011.

Green, James. *Death in the Haymarket: A Story of Chicago, the First Labor Movement, and the Bombing that Divided Gilded Age America*. New York: Pantheon Books, 2006.

# Bibliography

Gross, Robert A. *The Minutemen and Their World*. 25th ed. New York: Hill and Wang, 2001.

Halbrook, Stephen P. *Freedmen, the Fourteenth and the Right to Bear Arms, 1866–1876*. Santa Barbara, CA: Praeger, 1998.

Heier, Jan Richard. "Accounting for the Business of Suffering: A Study of the Antebellum Richmond, Virginia, Slave Trade." *Abacus* 40, no. 1 (March 2010): 60–83.

Hening, William Waller. *Hening's Statutes at Large, Being a Collection of All the Laws of Virginia from the First Session of the Legislature, in the Year 1619*. Vol I, 226. www.vagenweb.org/hening.

Horwitz, Tony. *Midnight Rising: John Brown and the Raid That Sparked the Civil War*. New York: Henry Holt and Company, 2011.

James, C.L.R. *Black Jacobins: Toussaint L'Ouverture and the San Domingo Revolution*. New York: Vintage Books, 1989.

Kelley, Robin D.G., and Earl Lewis, eds. *To Make This World Anew: A History of African Americans*. Vol. II. New York: Oxford University Press, 2005.

Lankford, Nelson. *Richmond Burning: The Last Days of the Confederate Capital*. New York: Viking, 2002.

Lanning, Michael Lee. *The Military 100: A Ranking of the Most Influential Leaders of All Time*. New York: Citadel Press, 2002.

Library of Congress. *Acts of the Second Congress of the United States, 1791–92*. www.loc.gov/law/help/statutes-at-large/2nd-congress/c2.pdf, accessed September 9, 2017.

Listman, John W. "Proud to Serve: Once Again in State Service." *Virginia GuardPost* (Winter 1995).

McInnis, Maurie D. "Mapping the Slave Trade in Richmond and New Orleans." *Buildings and Landscapes: Journal of Vernacular Architecture Forum* 20, no. 2 (Fall 2013): 102–25.

———. *Slaves Waiting for Sale: Abolitionist Art and the American Slave Trade*. Chicago: University of Chicago Press, 2011.

Rachleff, Peter. *Black Labor in Richmond, 1865–1890*. Urbana: University of Illinois Press, 1989.

Richardson, Heather Cox. "Reconstructing the Gilded Age and Progressive Era." In *A Companion to the Gilded Age and Progressive Era*, edited by Christopher M. Nichols and Nancy C. Unger. New York: Wiley Blackwell, 2017.

Richardson, Selden. Application to the U.S. Department of the Interior for the Leigh Street Armory to be placed in the National Register of Historic Places, August 2002.

———. *Built by Blacks: African American Architecture and Neighborhoods in Richmond, Virginia*. Charleston, SC: The History Press, 2008.

———. "Downtown Richmond's Phantom Armories: They Were Demolished Years Ago…Weren't They?" *Shockoe Examiner*, December 8, 2009. theshockoeexaminer.blogspot.com/2009/12/downtown-richmonds-phantom-armories.html.

Richmond School Board. *Minutes of Committee on Buildings and Furniture, 1899*. Richmond, VA, City of Richmond Archives.

Schwarz, Phillip J. *Gabriel's Conspiracy: A Documentary History*. Charlottesville: University of Virginia Press, 2012.

Tipple, John. "The Anatomy of Prejudice: Origins of the Robber Baron Legend." *Business History* 33, no. 4 (1959): 510–23.

Todd, Nancy L. *New York Historic Armories: An Illustrated History*. Albany: SUNY Press, 2006.

Trammell, Jack. *The Richmond Slave Trade: The Economic Backbone of the Old Dominion*. Charleston, SC: The History Press, 2012.

Twain, Mark, and Charles Dudley Warner. *The Gilded Age: A Tale of Today* (1873). Reprint. Fairfield, IA: 1st World Publishing, 2008.

United States War College. *An Examination of George Washington's Employment of Pennsylvania Militia at the Battle of Trenton and Princeton*. Scotts Valley, CA: CreateSpace, 2014.

Washington, George. "On Recruiting and Maintaining an Army 1776." American History: From Revolution to Reconstruction and beyond, 2012. www.let.rug.nl/usa/presidents/george-washington/on-recruiting-and-maintaining-an-army-1776.php.

Wilson, Adam P. *African American Army Officers of World War I: A Vanguard of Equality in War and Beyond*. Jefferson, NC: McFarland and Company, Inc., 2015.

Zinn, Howard. *A People's History of the United States*. Rev. ed. New York: HarperPerennial, 2015.

# Index

## A

Alexander, Ann Field
  on Croxton  102
  recruits rejected  94
Anderson, Carroll, Sr.  121
armories
  architectural features  42
  many were built  42
  New York's Seventh Regiment  42
  Richmond's armories  45

## B

black city councilmen  61
Black History Museum and Cultural Center of Virginia
  acquired the Armory  124
black militia
  Attucks Guard  27
  called to serve in Virginia  33
  in Virginia  26, 59
  "Negro militias"  60
  parades and ceremonies. *See* Mitchell, John, Jr.

black soldiers in America's wars  20
Blake, Alderman
  supports funding  69
Blues Armory
  built  45
  drill shed  73

## C

City of Richmond
  sold Armory to museum. *See* Leigh Street Armory
Constitution
  Confiscation and Militia Acts  21
  Emancipation Proclamation  21
  Fifteenth Amendment  90
  Fourteenth Amendment  26, 91
  Freedmen's Bureau  23
  militia  17
  Militia Acts, 1792  18
  militia assigned roles  18
  *Plessy v. Ferguson*  26
  Reconstruction Amendments  23
  Second Amendment  23
  state role with militia  18

# INDEX

Croxton, Colonel Richard C.
  appointed to command Sixth Virginia 91
  challenged Second Battalion officers 104
Cunningham, Roger D.
  black militia units called out 33
  state and guns for black militia 28
Cutshaw, Colonel W.E.
  background 80
  comments at turnover 83
  contributes to building Armory 61, 64
  recommends supplementary funding 68

## E

emancipation dates 36

## F

First African Baptist Church 40
First Battalion
  Band 38
  companies 28
  formed 28
  original armory 62
Fogelson, Roger M. 42

## G

Gilded Age
  Chicago's Haymarket Affair 49
  Mark Twain 46
  militias reorganized, armories built 50
  rapid change 46
  robber barons 46
  strikes, violence 46
Glasrud, Bruce A. 26

## H

Howitzer Armory
  built 45
  supplementary funding 72

## I

Immunes
  believed immune to tropical disease 108
  guard the Sixth Virginia 109
  mustered out 114

## J

Jim Crow 54, 75
Johnson, Major J.B.
  appointed major 28
  background 77
  comments at turnover 83
  contributes to building Armory 60, 66
  parading 41
  removes weapons from Sixth Virginia 110
  speaks to protesting troops 107
Johnson, Major R.H. 28
Johnson, Major W.H.
  appointed major 30
  resigns from Sixth Virginia 103

## L

Leigh Street Armory
  Armory stabilized. *See* Richardson, Selden
  bazaar 72
  celebrations at Armory 84
  center for recruitment and training for war 93
  construction approved 65
  drill shed 68
  fire 121
  funding for land 62

# Index

glowing in magnificent splendor 84
iconic physical symbol 58
location 64
masonry contract 74
official turnover 82
only nineteenth-century black armory 53
supplementary funding 68, 72
Virginia Museum for Black History and Archives, Inc. 121
why built in Richmond 59
women's club donates clock 86
Listman, John 93
officer issue affected decision about black regiment 28
on "First Battalion Infantry (Colored)" 28
ranks above major for black officers 93

## M

militia
 ineffective 15
 in the Constitution 17
 minutemen 15
 suppress slave uprisings 20
Mitchell, John, Jr.
 armory unique in American history 59
 background 75
 Blackman praises the *Planet* 113
 comments on masonry controversy 74
 construction of Armory 61, 66
 gives credit to Major Johnson 64
 hoped for a drill shed 68
 Knights of Pythias 36, 38
 no officers, no fight 90
 parades and ceremonies 35
 *Richmond Planet* 36
 writes history of Armory 58
Mitchell, Thomas W.
 John's brother falls from horse 40
Monroe Center
 new name for Armory. *See* Richmond Public Schools

soldiers use the center during World War II 119

## P

Palmer, Major William H. 30

## R

Richardson, Selden
 Armory stabilized 124
 Cutshaw's role with Armory 80
 National Register of Historic Places 121
 OCD remodels Armory 119
Richmond Public Schools
 approve conversion of Armory to a school 117
 Armory becomes the Monroe Center 119
 city council approves the conversion 118
 Monroe Elementary, Armstrong High, Graves Middle, Colored Special 121
 OCD adds a gymnasium 119
*Richmond Times Dispatch* 84
Richmond, Virginia
 slave trade 56
Robert E. Lee Monument 41

## S

Second Battalion
 companies 30
 formed 28
 majors 30
Spanish-American War
 "A. Blackman" defends the Sixth, praises the *Planet* 113
 "A. Blackman" writes from Camp Haskill 112
 black officers approved 94

# INDEX

black soldiers believe white officers biased  105
black troops fail physicals  94
black troops form "Council of Uglies"  111
black troops mustered out  114
Camp Corbin  97
Camp Haskill  108
Camp Poland  100
"Ham" reports from camp  97
McKinley, President William  88
most rights restored at Camp Haskill  112
"Mutinous Sixth"  114
railroad tracks laid into Camp Haskill  114
Second Battalion credentials challenged  100
Second Battalion officers resign and mustered out  106
Sixth Virginia restricted at Camp Haskill  109
Tenth Regiment of Immunes mustered out  114
USS *Maine* explosion  88
weapons removed from Sixth Virginia  110
white officers replace black officers  107

## T

Taylor, Mayor Richmond M.  68
Tyler, Governor James Hoge
  relents and appoints black battalion officers  92
  resists appointing black officers  88

## V

Virginia
  denies blacks access to weapons, 1640  19
  irony of a black armory  54
  Point Comfort, Fort Monroe  55
  role in Civil War  55
  slavery  55
  slave trade  55

## W

Walker, Armistead  73
Washington, George
  adjutant general of Virginia Militia  15
  misgivings about militia  16

# About the Authors

ROICE D. LUKE, PHD, is professor emeritus, Virginia Commonwealth University, where from 1982 to 2011 he served as chair and then professor in the Department of Health Administration. From 2005 to 2009, he led locally the Virginia Freedmen's Bureau Digitization and Extraction Project, in collaboration with the Black History Museum and Cultural Center of Virginia (BHM), Family Search and NARA. From 2008 to 2015, he served on the BHM board. He has numerous publications on healthcare policy and corporate strategy and has authored a number of op-eds, published in the *Richmond Times Dispatch*, connecting African American history and public policy.

*Corey Miller Photography.*

MAUREEN ELGERSMAN LEE, DAH, served as executive director of the Black History Museum and Cultural Center of Virginia from 2008 to 2013 and is currently an associate professor of history and chair of the Department of Political Science and History at Hampton University in Hampton, Virginia. A graduate of Redeemer University College in Ancaster, Ontario, and Clark Atlanta

University in Atlanta, Georgia, Dr. Elgersman Lee's publications include *Unyielding Spirits: Black Women and Slavery in Early Canada and Jamaica* and *Black Bangor: African Americans in a Maine Community, 1880–1950*.

STACY LEE BURRS has an undergraduate degree from the University of North Carolina at Fayetteville and has done graduate work at the New School for social research. He has worked with a diverse group of local, state and national organizations, including the National Office of the United Negro College Fund, State Office of Minority Business Enterprise, the City of Richmond, Venture Richmond and many others. He has also served on a number of other important boards and committees in the region. He has served as CEO, chairman and board member of the Black History Museum and Cultural Center of Virginia, in which capacity he led the effort to acquire, renovate and convert to a museum the historic Leigh Street Armory.